LEARN TO

Crochet in a Day

Bootie Boutique, page 84

www.companyscoming.com
visit our ↑ website

Learn to Crochet in a Day

First Printing April 2010

Library and Archives Canada Cataloguing in Publication
Learn to crochet in a day.
(Workshop series)
Includes index.
ISBN 978-1-897477-38-0
1. Crocheting. 2. Crocheting--Patterns.
I. Title: Crochet in a day. II. Series: Workshop series (Edmonton, Alta.)
TT820.L424 2010   746.43'4   C2009-904824-8

Published by
Company's Coming Publishing Limited
2311-96 Street
Edmonton, Alberta, Canada T6N 1G3
Tel: 780-450-6223 Fax: 780-450-1857
www.companyscoming.com

Company's Coming is a registered trademark owned by Company's Coming Publishing Limited

Printed in China

The Company's Coming Story

Jean Paré grew up with an understanding that family, friends and home cooking are the key ingredients for a good life. A mother of four, Jean worked as a professional caterer for 18 years, operating out of her home kitchen. During that time, she came to appreciate quick and easy recipes that call for everyday ingredients. In answer to mounting requests for her recipes, Company's Coming cookbooks were born, and Jean moved on to a new chapter in her career.

In the beginning, Jean worked from a spare bedroom in her home, located in the small prairie town of Vermilion, Alberta, Canada. The first Company's Coming cookbook, *150 Delicious Squares*, was an immediate bestseller. Today, with well over 150 titles in print, Company's Coming has earned the distinction of publishing Canada's most popular cookbooks. The company continues to gain new supporters by adhering to Jean's "Golden Rule of Cooking"—Never share a recipe you wouldn't use yourself. It's an approach that has worked—millions of times over!

Company's Coming cookbooks are distributed throughout Canada, the United States, Australia and other international English-language markets. French and Spanish language editions have also been published. Sales to date have surpassed 25 million copies with no end in sight. Familiar and trusted in home kitchens around the world, Company's Coming cookbooks are highly regarded both as kitchen workbooks and as family heirlooms.

Company's Coming founder Jean Paré

Just as Company's Coming continues to promote the tradition of home cooking, the same is now true with crafting. Like good cooking, great craft results depend upon easy-to-follow instructions, readily available materials and enticing photographs of the finished products. Also like cooking, crafting is meant to be enjoyed in the home or cottage. Company's Coming Crafts, then, is a natural extension from the kitchen into the family room or den.

Because Company's Coming operates a test kitchen and not a craft shop, we've partnered with a major North American craft content publisher to assemble a variety of craft compilations exclusively for us. Our editors have been involved every step of the way. You can see the excellent results for yourself in the book you're holding.

Company's Coming Crafts are for everyone—whether you're a beginner or a seasoned pro. What better gift could you offer than something you've made yourself? In these hectic days, people still enjoy crafting parties; they bring family and friends together in the same way a good meal does. Company's Coming is proud to support crafters with this new creative book series.

We hope you enjoy these easy-to-follow, informative and colourful books, and that they inspire your creativity. So, don't delay—get crafty!

TABLE OF CONTENTS

Foreword 7 • Crochet Basics 8

Fabulous Fashions & Accessories

Create a wardrobe full of these fun designs using a variety of yarns.

Fabulous Felted Tote, page 48

Easy Tie Wrap, page 51

Glorious Gifts

Stitch a special gift that will truly be treasured by family and friends.

Spa Set, page 66

TABLE OF CONTENTS

Heartfelt Home Decor

Decorate your home with these easy projects that add a special touch to any room.

Classy Cables Pillow, page 100

Sea Breeze Table Runner, page 92

Towel Edgings, page 118

Country Lace Afghan, page 103

Make it yourself!

COMPANY'S COMING
CRAFT WORKSHOP BOOKS

LEARN TO Sew for the Table
48 easy-to-make projects
Step-by-step instructions
Colour photos of every project

LEARN TO Knit for Baby

Kids LEARN TO Knit, Quilt & Crochet
27 easy-to-make projects
Step-by-step instructions
Colour photos of every project

LEARN TO Quilt With Panels

LEARN TO Knit in the Round

LEARN TO Make Cards With Photos
48 easy-to-make projects
Step-by-step instructions

LEARN TO Craft With Paper

LEARN TO Bead Jewellery
89 easy-to-make projects
Step-by-step instructions
Colour photos of every project

CRAFT WORKSHOP SERIES

Get a craft class in a book! General instructions
teach basic skills or how to apply them in a new
way. Easy-to-follow steps, diagrams and photos
make projects simple.

Whether paper crafting, knitting, crocheting,
beading, sewing or quilting—find beautiful, fun
designs you can make yourself.

For a complete listing of Company's Coming cookbooks and craft books, check out
www.companyscoming.com

FOREWORD

Learn the basic techniques of crochet in 12 easy lessons! You'll learn all the basic stitches with the help of step-by-step instructions and colourful illustrations, plus find great tips on yarn types, hook sizes, how to check your gauge and how to read patterns. You'll also find lessons in working with colours and finishing your items. After you master the basics it will be hard to choose which project to stitch first, with over 30 designs to choose from!

Choose between fashion and accessory designs including a classic hat and scarf, an easy tie wrap, a fringed shell skirt and an easy summer top—all fun and fabulous designs that will complement your wardrobe. All are yours to create from a variety of colourful yarns!

Stitch gift items such as bookmarks, baby booties or a spa set, and watch the recipient's face light up when your homemade gift is opened. By learning to crochet, you will be able to make wonderful gifts treasured by all.

If you are looking for new ways to decorate your home, the home decor chapter offers great options such as Simply Sweet Doilies, a Harvest Rug or a Classy Cables Pillow—just a few of the many wonderful projects to choose from. From kitchen to bath and every room in between, you'll find an easy crocheted design to add that special touch.

Once you've mastered these basic techniques, you will be on your way to being a crocheting expert—the variety of stitches and patterns you can create with these basic skills are endless. Be daring and you'll find you can mix stitch patterns for even more variety. You can make everything from coasters to covers to clothing! Let your imagination run wild and learn to crochet today.

Pastel Shells Afghan, page 81

CROCHET BASICS

Fringed Shell Skirt, page 58

Yarns

Both yarn and crochet cottons come in many sizes, from the fine crochet cotton used for doilies, to the wonderful bulky mohair used for afghans and sweaters. The most commonly used yarn is medium (or worsted) weight. It is readily available in a wide variety of beautiful colours. This is the weight we will use in our lessons. Always read yarn labels carefully. The label will tell you how much yarn, in ounces, grams, metres and/or yards, is in the skein or ball. Read the label to find out the fibre content of the yarn, its washability, and sometimes, how to pull the yarn from the skein. Also, there is usually a dye-lot number on the label. This number assures you that the colour of each skein with this number is the same. Yarn of the same colour name may vary in shade somewhat from dye lot to dye lot, creating variations in colour when a project is completed. Therefore, when purchasing yarn for a project, it is important to match the dye-lot numbers on the skeins.

Tapestry Needle

You'll need a tapestry needle, a blunt-pointed sewing needle with an eye big enough to carry the yarn, for weaving in yarn ends and sewing seams. This is a size 16 steel tapestry needle. You can buy big plastic needles called yarn needles, but they are not as good as the steel needles.

Gauge

Gauge is the single most important factor in crochet. If you don't work to gauge, your crocheted projects may not be the correct size, and you may not have enough yarn to finish your project.

Gauge means the number of stitches per inch, and rows per inch, that result from a specified yarn worked with a specified-size hook. Since everyone crochets differently—loosely, tightly or in-between—the measurements of individual work can vary greatly even when using the same-size hook and yarn. It is your responsibility to make sure you achieve the gauge specified in the pattern.

Hook sizes given in the materials are merely guides and should never be used without making a 4-inch-square sample swatch to check gauge. Make the sample gauge swatch using the size hook, yarn and stitch specified in the pattern. If you have more stitches per inch than specified, try again using a larger-size hook. If you have fewer stitches per inch than specified, try again using a smaller-size hook. Do not hesitate to change to a larger- or smaller-size hook, if necessary, to achieve gauge.

If you have the correct number of stitches per inch, but cannot achieve the row gauge, adjust the height of your stitches. This means that after inserting the hook to begin a new stitch, draw up a little more yarn if your stitches are not tall enough—this makes the first loop slightly higher—or draw up less yarn if your stitches are too tall. Practice will help you achieve the correct height.

This photo shows how to measure your gauge:

Reading Patterns

Crochet patterns are written in a special language full of abbreviations, asterisks, parentheses, brackets and other symbols and terms. These short forms are used so instructions will not take up too much space. They may seem confusing at first, but once understood, they are easy to follow.

Abbreviations

beg begin/begins/beginning
bpdc back post double crochet
bpsc back post single crochet
bptr back post treble crochet
CC contrasting colour
ch(s) chain stitch(es)
ch- refers to chain or space previously made (i.e. ch-1 space)
ch sp(s) chain space(s)
cl(s) cluster(s)
cm centimetre(s)
dc double crochet (singular/plural)
dc dec double crochet 2 or more stitches together, as indicated
dec decrease/decreases/decreasing
dtr double treble crochet
ext extended
fpdc front post double crochet
fpsc front post single crochet
fptr front post treble crochet
g gram(s)
hdc half double crochet
hdc dec half double crochet 2 or more stitches together, as indicated
inc increase/increases/increasing
lp(s) loops(s)

MC main colour
mm millimetre(s)
oz ounce(s)
pc popcorn(s)
rem remain/remains/remaining
rep(s) repeat(s)
rnd(s) round(s)
RS right side
sc single crochet
sc dec single crochet 2 or more stitches together, as indicated
sk skip/skipped/skipping
sl st(s) slip stitch(es)
sp(s) space(s)/spaced
st(s) stitch(es)
tog together
tr treble crochet
trtr triple treble crochet
WS wrong side
yd(s) yard(s)
yo yarn over

Symbols

* **An asterisk** is used to mark the beginning of a portion of instructions which will be worked more than once; thus, "rep from * twice" means after working the instructions once, repeat the instructions following the asterisk twice more (3 times in all).

[ ] Brackets are used to enclose instructions which should be repeated the number of times specified immediately following the brackets: "[2 sc in next dc, sc in next dc] twice." Brackets are also used to indicate additional or clarifying information for multiple sizes: "child's size 2 [4, 6]"; "Row 29 [31, 33]."

( ) Parentheses are used to set off and clarify a group of stitches that are to be worked all into the same space or stitch, such as: "in corner sp work (2 dc, ch 1, 2 dc)."

{ } Braces are used to indicate a set of repeat instructions within a bracketed or parenthetical set of repeat instructions: "[{ch 5, sc in next ch sp} twice, ch 5, sk next dc]"; "({dc, ch 1} 5 times, dc) in next ch sp)."

Terms

Front loop (front lp) is the loop toward you at the top of the stitch (Figure 1).

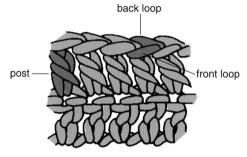

Figure 1

Back loop (back lp) is the loop away from you at the top of the stitch (Figure 1).

Post is the vertical part of the stitch (Figure 1).

Wrong side (WS): the side of the work that will not show when project is in use.

Right side (RS): the side that will show.

Right-hand side: the side nearest your right hand as you are working.

Left-hand side: the side nearest your left hand as you are working.

Right front: the piece of a garment that will be worn on the right-hand side of the body.

Left front: the piece of a garment that will be worn on the left-hand side of the body.

How To Hold Your Hook

Crochet hooks come in many sizes, from very fine steel hooks used to make intricate doilies and lace, to very large ones of plastic or wood used to make bulky sweaters or rugs.

The hooks you will use most often are made of aluminum, are about 6 inches long and are sized alphabetically by letter from B (the smallest) to K. For our lessons, you'll need a size H hook, which is a medium size.

The aluminum crochet hook looks like this:

In Figure 1, (A) is the hook end, which is used to hook the yarn and draw it through other loops of yarn (called stitches). (B) is the throat, a shaped area that helps you slide the stitch up onto (C) the working area. (D) is the fingerhold, a flattened area that helps you grip the hook comfortably, usually with your thumb and third finger; and (E) is the handle, which rests under your fourth and little fingers, and provides balance for easy, smooth work.

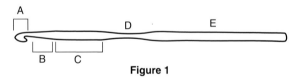

Figure 1

It is important that every stitch is made on the working area, never on the throat (which would make the stitch too tight) and never on the fingerhold (which would stretch the stitch).

The hook is held in the right hand, with the thumb and third finger on the fingerhold, and the index finger near the tip of the hook (Figure 2).

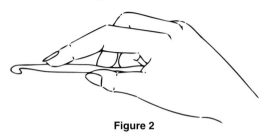

Figure 2

The hook should be turned slightly toward you, not facing up or down. Figure 3 shows how the hook is held, viewing from underneath the hand. The hook should be held firmly, but not tightly.

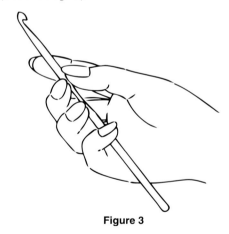

Figure 3

Lesson 1: Chain Stitch (ch)

Crochet usually begins with a series of chain stitches called a beginning, starting or foundation chain. Begin by making a slip knot on the hook about 6 inches from the free end of the yarn. Loop the yarn as shown in Figure 4.

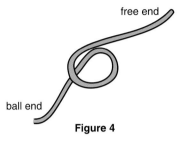

Figure 4

Insert the hook through centre of loop and hook the free end (Figure 5).

Figure 5

Pull the free end through the loop and up onto the working area of the hook (Figure 6).

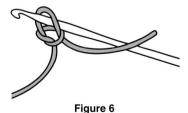

Figure 6

Pull the free yarn end to tighten the loop (Figure 7).

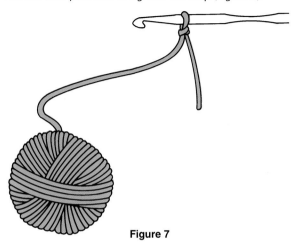

Figure 7

The loop should be firm, but loose enough to slide back and forth easily on the hook. Be sure you still have about a 6-inch yarn end.

Hold the hook, now with its slip knot, in your right hand (Figure 8).

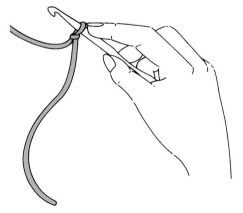

Figure 8

Now let's make the first chain stitch.

1. Hold the base of the slip knot with the thumb and index finger of your left hand, and thread yarn from the skein over the middle finger (Figure 9) and under the remaining fingers of the left hand (Figure 9a).

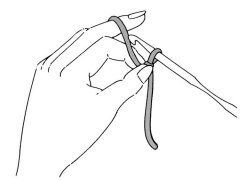

Figure 9

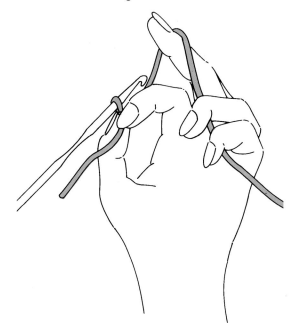

Figure 9a

Your middle finger will stick up a bit to help the yarn feed smoothly from the skein; the other fingers help maintain even tension on the yarn as you work.

Tip: As you practice, you can adjust the way your left hand holds the yarn or thread to however is most comfortable for you.

2. Bring the yarn over the hook from back to front and hook it (Figure 10).

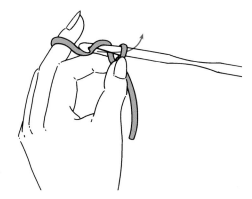

Figure 10

Draw hooked yarn through the loop of the slip knot on the hook and up onto the working area of the hook *(see arrow on Figure 10)*; you have now made one chain stitch (Figure 11).

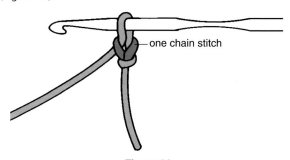

one chain stitch

Figure 11

Crochet Basics | *Learn to Crochet in a Day*

3. Again bring the yarn over the hook from back to front (Figure 12a).

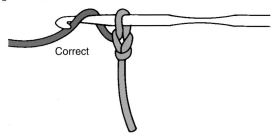

Figure 12a

Tip: Take care not to bring yarn from front to back (Figure 12b).

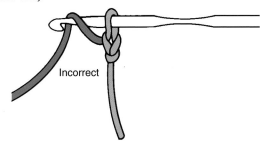

Figure 12b

Hook it and draw through loop on the hook—you have made another chain stitch (Figure 13).

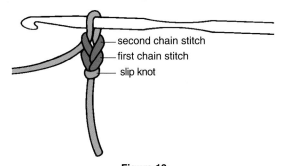

— second chain stitch
— first chain stitch
— slip knot

Figure 13

Repeat Step 3 for each additional chain stitch, being careful to move the left thumb and index finger up the chain close to the hook after each new stitch or two (Figure 14a). This helps you control the work.

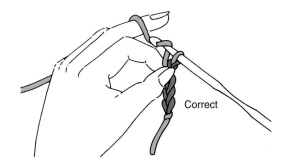

Figure 14a

Tip: Figure 14b shows the incorrect way to hold the stitches. Also be sure to pull each new stitch up onto the working area of the hook.

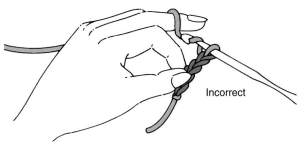

Figure 14b

The working yarn and the work in progress are always held in your left hand.

Practice making chains until you are comfortable with your grip of the hook and the flow of the yarn. In the beginning your work will be uneven, with some chain stitches loose and others tight. While you're learning, try to keep the chain stitches loose. As your skill increases, the chain should be firm, but not tight, with all chain stitches even in size.

Tip: As you practice, if the hook slips out of a stitch, don't get upset! Just insert the hook again from the front into the centre of the last stitch, taking care not to twist the loop (Figure 15).

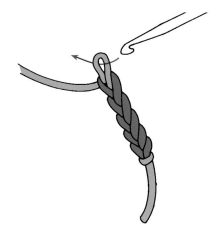

Figure 15

When you are comfortable with the chain stitch, draw your hook out of the last stitch and pull out the work back to the beginning. Now you've learned the important first step of crochet: the beginning or foundation chain.

Lesson 2: Working Into the Chain

Once you have worked the beginning chain, you are ready to begin the stitches required to make any project. These stitches are worked into the foundation chain. For practice, make six chains loosely.

Tip: When counting your chain stitches at the start of a pattern—which you must do very carefully before continuing—note that the loop on the hook is never counted as a stitch, and the starting slip knot is never counted as a stitch (Figure 16).

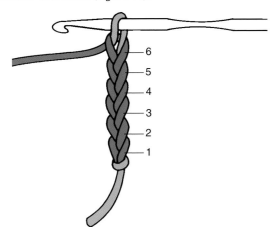

Figure 16

Now stop and look at the chain. The front looks like a series of interlocking "V"s (Figure 16), and each stitch has a bump or ridge at the back (Figure 17).

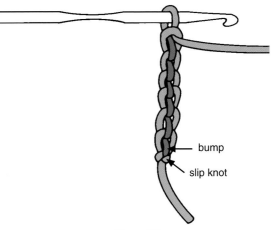

Figure 17

You will never work into the first chain from the hook. Depending on the stitch, you will work into the second, third, fourth, etc., chain from the hook. The instructions will always state how many chains to skip before starting the first stitch.

When working a stitch, insert hook from the front of the chain, through the centre of a "V" at the top of the chain and under the corresponding bump on the back of the same chain (Figure 18).

Excluding the first stitch, you will work into every stitch in the chain unless the pattern states differently, but not into the starting slip knot (Figure 18a). Be sure that you do not skip that last chain at the end.

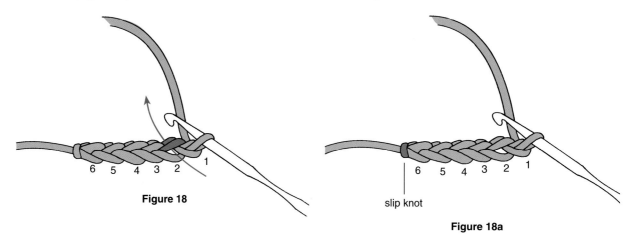

Figure 18

Figure 18a

Lesson 3: Single Crochet (sc)

Most crochet is made with variations on just four different stitches: single crochet, double crochet, half double crochet and treble crochet. The stitches differ mainly in height, which is varied by the number of times the yarn is wrapped around the hook. The shortest and most basic of these stitches is the single crochet.

Working Row 1

To practice, begin with the chain of six stitches made in Lesson 3 and work the first row of single crochet as follows:

1. Skip first chain stitch from hook. Insert hook in the second chain stitch through the centre of the "V" and under the back bump; with third finger of your left hand, bring yarn over the hook from back to front, and hook the yarn (Figure 19).

Figure 19

Draw yarn through the chain stitch and well up onto the working area of the hook. You now have two loops on the hook (Figure 20).

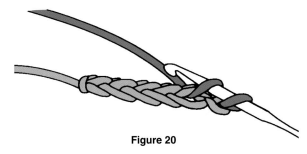

Figure 20

2. Again, bring yarn over the hook from back to front, hook the yarn and draw it through both loops on the hook (Figure 21).

Figure 21

One loop will remain on the hook, and you have made one single crochet (Figure 22).

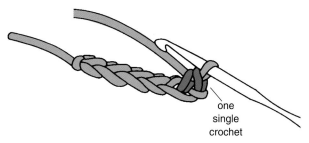

Figure 22

3. Insert hook in next chain stitch as before, hook the yarn and draw it through the chain stitch; hook the yarn again and draw it through both loops: You have made another single crochet.

Repeat Step 3 in each remaining chain stitch, taking care to work in the last chain stitch, but not in the slip knot. You have completed one row of single crochet, and should have five stitches in the row. Figure 23 shows how to count the stitches.

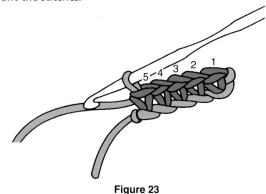

Figure 23

Tip: As you work, be careful not to twist the chain; keep all the "V"s facing you.

Working Row 2

To work the second row of single crochet, you need to turn the work in the direction of the arrow (counterclockwise), as shown in Figure 24, so you can work back across the first row.

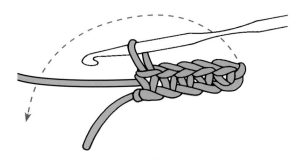

Figure 24

Do not remove the hook from the loop as you do this (Figure 24a).

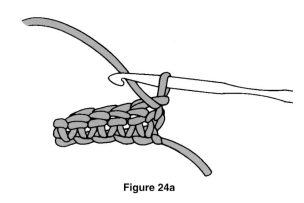

Figure 24a

Now you need to bring the yarn up to the correct height to work the first stitch. So, to raise the yarn, chain one (this is called a beginning chain).

This row, and all the following rows of single crochet, will be worked into a previous row of single crochet, not into the starting chain as you did before. Remember that when you worked into the starting chain, you inserted the hook through the centre of the "V" and under the bump. This is only done when working into a starting chain.

To work into a previous row of crochet, insert the hook under both loops of the previous stitch, as shown in Figure 25, instead of through the centre of the "V".

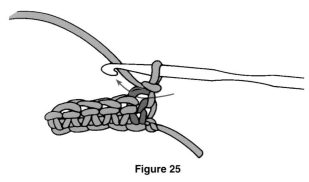

Figure 25

The first single crochet of the row is worked in the last stitch of the previous row (Figure 25), not into the beginning chain. Work a single crochet into each single crochet to the end, taking care to work in each stitch, especially the last stitch, which is easy to miss (Figure 26).

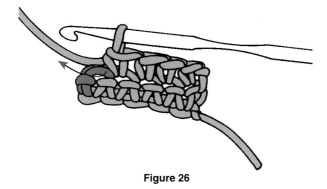

Figure 26

Stop now and count your stitches; you should still have five single crochet on the row (Figure 27).

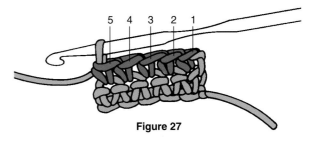

Figure 27

Tip: When you want to pause to count stitches, check your work, have a snack or chat on the phone, you can remove your hook from the work—but do this at the end of a row, not in the middle. To remove the hook, pull straight up on the hook to make a long loop (Figure 28). Then withdraw the hook and put it on a table or other safe place (sofas and chairs have a habit of eating crochet hooks). Put work in a safe place so loop is not pulled out. To begin work again, just insert the hook in the big loop (don't twist the loop), and pull on the yarn from the skein to tighten the loop.

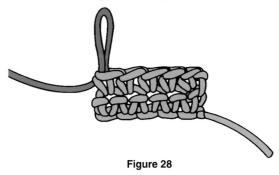

Figure 28

To end row two, after the last single crochet, turn the work counterclockwise.

Here is the way instructions for row two might be written in a pattern:

Note: To save space, a number of abbreviations are used. For a list of abbreviations used in patterns, see page 10.

Row 2: Ch 1, sc in each sc, turn.

Working Row 3

Row 3 is worked exactly as you worked row 2. Here are the instructions as they would be given in a pattern:

Row 3: Rep row 2.

Now wasn't that easy? For practice, work three more rows, which means you will repeat row 2 three times more.

Tip: Try to keep your stitches as smooth and even as possible; remember to work loosely rather than tightly and to make each stitch well up on the working area of the hook. Be sure to turn at the end of each row and to check carefully to be sure you've worked into the last stitch of each row.

Count the stitches at the end of each row; do you still have five? Good work.

Tip: What if you don't have five stitches at the end of a row? Perhaps you worked two stitches in one stitch or skipped a stitch. Find your mistake, then just pull out your stitches back to the mistake. Pulling out in crochet is simple—just take out the hook and gently pull on the yarn. The stitches will come out easily; when you reach the place where you want to start again, insert the hook in the last loop (taking care not to twist it) and begin.

Fastening Off

It's time to move on to another stitch, so let's fasten off your single crochet practice piece, which you can keep for future reference. After the last stitch of the last row, cut the yarn, leaving a 6-inch end. As you did when you took your hook out for a break, draw the hook straight up, but this time draw the cut end of the yarn completely through the stitch. Photo A shows an actual sample of six rows of single crochet to which you can compare your practice rows. It also shows how to count the stitches and rows.

Photo A

Now you can put the piece away, and it won't pull out (you might want to tag this piece as a sample of single crochet).

Lesson 4: Double Crochet (dc)

Double crochet is a taller stitch than single crochet. To practice, first chain 14 stitches loosely. Then work the first row of double crochet as follows:

Working Row 1

1. Bring yarn once over the hook from back to front (as though you were going to make another chain stitch); skip the first three chains from the hook, then insert hook in the fourth chain (Figure 29).

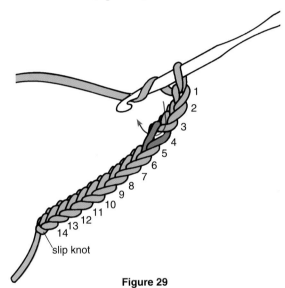

Figure 29

Remember not to count the loop on the hook as a chain. Be sure to go through the centre of the "V" of the chain and under the bump at the back, and do not twist the chain.

2. Hook yarn and draw it through the chain stitch and up onto the working area of the hook: you now have three loops on the hook (Figure 30).

Figure 30

3. Hook yarn and draw through the first 2 loops on the hook (Figure 31).

Figure 31

You now have 2 loops on the hook (Figure 32).

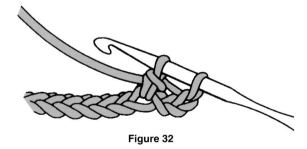

Figure 32

4. Hook yarn and draw through both loops on the hook (Figure 33).

Figure 33

You have now completed one double crochet and one loop remains on the hook (Figure 34).

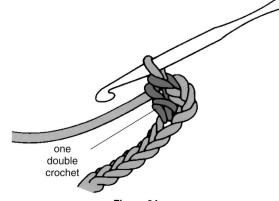

one
double
crochet

Figure 34

Repeat Steps 1 through 4 in each chain stitch across (except in Step 1, work in next chain; don't skip three chains).

When you've worked a double crochet in the last chain, pull out your hook and look at your work. Then count your double crochet stitches: there should be 12 of them, counting the first three chain stitches you skipped at the beginning of the row as a double crochet (Figure 35).

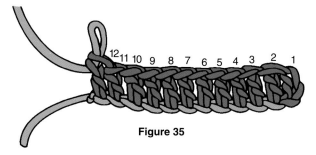

Figure 35

Tip: In working double crochet on a beginning chain row, the three chains skipped before making the first double crochet are always counted as a double crochet stitch.

Turn the work counterclockwise before beginning row 2.

Working Row 2

To work row 2, you need to bring the yarn up to the correct height for the next row. To raise the yarn, chain three (this is called the beginning chain).

The three chains in the beginning chain just made count as the first double crochet of the new row, so skip the first double crochet and work a double crochet in the second stitch. Be sure to insert the hook under the top two loops of the stitch: Figures 36a and 36b indicate the correct and incorrect placement of this stitch.

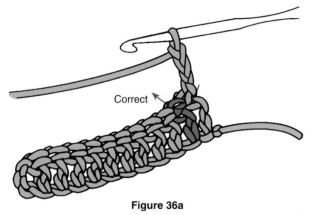

Figure 36a

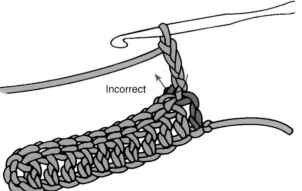

Figure 36b

Work a double crochet in each remaining stitch across the previous row; at the end of each row, be sure to work the last double crochet in the top of the beginning chain from the previous row. Be sure to insert hook in the centre of the "V" (and back bump) of the top chain of the beginning chain (Figure 37). Stop and count your double crochet; there should be 12 stitches. Now, turn the rows.

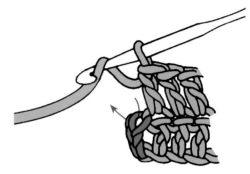

Figure 37

Here is the way the instructions might be written in a pattern:

Row 2: Ch 3, dc in each dc across, turn. *(12 dc)*

Working Row 3

Row 3 is worked exactly as you worked row 2.

In a pattern, instructions would read:

Row 3: Rep row 2.

For practice, work three more rows, repeating row 2. At the end of the last row, fasten off the yarn as you did for the single crochet practice piece. Photo B shows a sample of six rows of double crochet and how to count the stitches and rows.

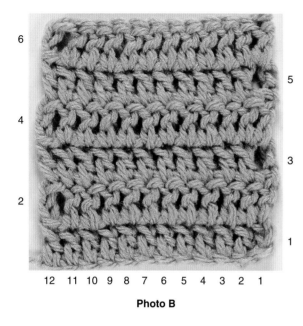

Photo B

Break Time!

Now you have learned the two most-often-used stitches in crochet. Since you've worked so hard, it's time to take a break. Walk around, relax your hands, have a snack or just take a few minutes to release the stress that sometimes develops when learning something new.

Lesson 5: Half Double Crochet (hdc)

Just as its name implies, this stitch eliminates one step of double crochet and works up about half as tall.

To practice, chain 13 stitches loosely.

Working Row 1

1. Bring yarn once over hook from back to front, skip the first two chains, then insert hook in the third chain from the hook (Figure 38).

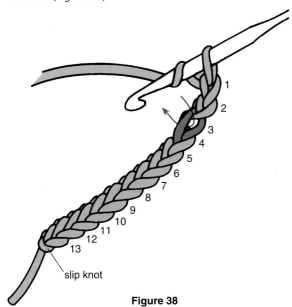

Figure 38

Remember not to count the loop on the hook as a chain.

2. Hook yarn and draw it through the chain stitch and up onto the working area of the hook. You now have three loops on the hook (Figure 39).

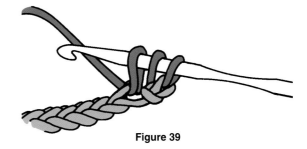

Figure 39

3. Hook yarn and draw it through all three loops on the hook in one motion (Figure 40).

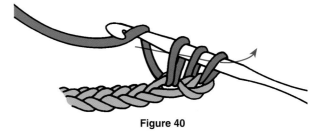

Figure 40

You have completed one half double crochet and one loop remains on the hook (Figure 41).

Figure 41

In next chain stitch, work a half double crochet as follows:

1. Bring yarn once over hook from back to front, insert hook in next chain.

2. Hook yarn and draw it through the chain stitch and up onto the working area of the hook. You now have three loops on the hook.

3. Hook yarn and draw it through all three loops on the hook in one motion.

Repeat the previous three steps in each remaining chain stitch across. Stop and count your stitches: You should have 12 half double crochet, counting the first two chains you skipped at the beginning of the row as a half double crochet (Figure 42).

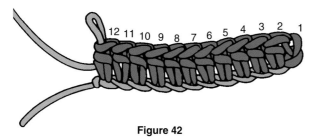

Figure 42

Turn your work.

Working Row 2

Like double crochet, the beginning chain counts as a stitch in half double crochet (unless your pattern specifies otherwise). Chain two, skip the first half double crochet of the previous row and work a half double crochet in the second stitch (Figure 43) and in each remaining stitch across the previous row. At the end of the row, turn.

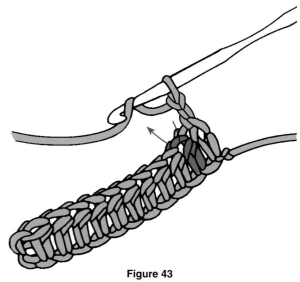

Figure 43

Here is the way the instructions might be written in a pattern:

Row 2: Ch 2, hdc in each hdc across, turn. *(12 hdc)*

Working Row 3

Row 3 is worked exactly as you worked row 2.

For practice, work three more rows, repeating row 2. Be sure to count your stitches carefully at the end of each row. When the practice rows are completed, fasten off. Photo C shows a sample of six rows of half double crochet and how to count the stitches and the rows. Continue with the next lesson.

Photo C

Lesson 6: Treble Crochet (tr)

Treble crochet is a tall stitch that works up quickly and is fun to do. To practice, first chain 15 stitches loosely. Then work the first row as follows:

Working Row 1

1. Bring yarn twice over the hook (from back to front), skip the first four chains, then insert hook into the fifth chain from the hook (Figure 44).

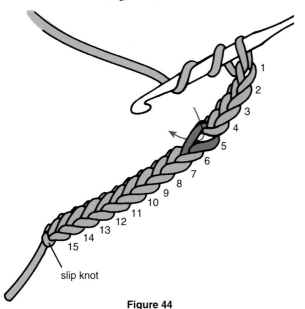

slip knot

Figure 44

2. Hook yarn and draw it through the chain stitch and up onto the working area of the hook; you now have four loops on the hook (Figure 45).

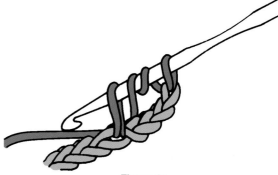

Figure 45

3. Hook yarn and draw it through the first two loops on the hook (Figure 46).

Figure 46

You now have three loops on the hook (Figure 46a).

Figure 46a

4. Hook yarn again and draw it through the next two loops on the hook (Figure 47).

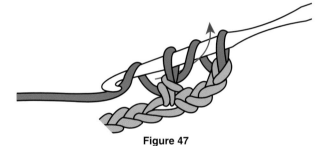

Figure 47

Two loops remain on the hook (Figure 47a).

Figure 47a

5. Hook yarn and draw it through both remaining loops on the hook (Figure 48).

Figure 48

You have now completed one treble crochet and one loop remains on the hook (Figure 49).

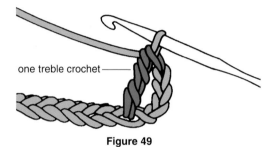

one treble crochet —

Figure 49

In next chain stitch work a treble crochet as follows:

1. Bring yarn twice over the hook (from back to front); insert hook in the next chain (Figure 50).

Figure 50

2. Hook yarn and draw it through the chain stitch and up onto the working area of the hook; you now have four loops on the hook.

3. Hook yarn and draw it through the first two loops on the hook.

You now have three loops on the hook.

4. Hook yarn again and draw it through the next two loops on the hook.

Two loops remain on the hook.

5. Hook yarn and draw it through both remaining loops on the hook.

Repeat the previous five steps in each remaining chain stitch across.

When you've worked a treble crochet in the last chain, count your stitches: there should be 12 of them, counting the first four chains you skipped at the beginning of the row as a treble crochet (Figure 51); turn work.

Figure 51

Tip: In working the first row of treble crochet, the four chains skipped before making the first treble crochet are always counted as a treble crochet stitch.

Working Row 2

Chain four to bring your yarn up to the correct height, and to count as the first stitch of the row. Skip the first stitch and work a treble crochet in the second stitch (Figure 52).

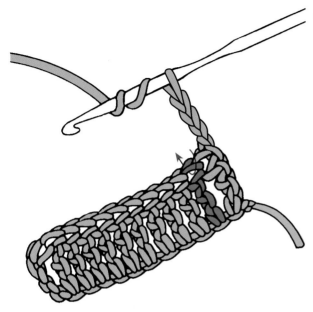

Figure 52

Work a treble crochet in each remaining stitch across previous row; be sure to work last treble crochet in the top of the beginning chain from the previous row. Count stitches: be sure you still have 12 stitches; turn work.

Tip: Remember to work last treble crochet of each row in beginning chain of previous row. Missing this stitch in the beginning chain is a common error.

Here is the way the instructions might be written in a pattern:

Row 2: Ch 4, tr in each tr across, turn. *(12 tr)*

Working Row 3

Work row 3 exactly as you worked row 2.

For practice, work three more rows, repeating row 2. At the end of the last row, fasten off the yarn. Photo D shows a sample of six rows of treble crochet and how to count the stitches and rows.

Photo D

Lesson 7: Slip Stitch (sl st)

This is the shortest of all crochet stitches and is really more a technique than a stitch. Slip stitches are usually used to move yarn across a group of stitches without adding height, or they may be used to join different part of a project.

Moving Yarn Across Stitches
Chain 10.

Working Row 1
Double crochet in the fourth chain from hook (see page 23) and in each chain across. Turn work. On the next row, you are going to slip stitch across the first four stitches before beginning to work double crochet again.

Working Row 2
Instead of making three chains for the beginning chain as you would usually do for a second row of double crochet, this time just chain one. The beginning chain-one does not count as a stitch; therefore, insert hook under both loops of first stitch, hook yarn and draw it through both loops of stitch and loop on the hook (Figure 53): one slip stitch made.

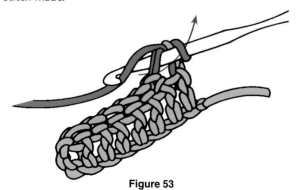

Figure 53

Work a slip stitch in the same manner in each of the next three stitches. Now we're going to finish the row in double crochet; chain three to get yarn at the right height (the chain three counts as a double crochet), then work a double crochet in each of the remaining stitches. Look at your work and see how we moved the thread across with slip stitches, adding very little height (Figure 54).

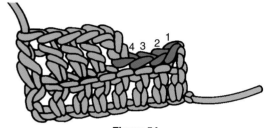

Figure 54

Fasten off and save the sample.

Here is the way the instructions might be written in a pattern.

Row 2: Ch 1, sl st in each of first 4 dc, ch 3, dc in each rem dc across, turn. *(5 dc)*

Fasten off.

Tip: When slip stitching across stitches, always work very loosely.

Joining Stitches

Joining a Chain Into a Circle
Chain six, then insert hook through the first chain you made (next to the slip knot—Figure 55).

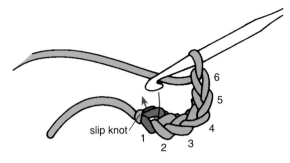

Figure 55

Hook yarn and draw it through the chain and through the loop on hook; you have now joined the six chains into a circle or a ring. This is the way many motifs, such as granny squares, are started. Cut yarn and keep this practice piece as a sample.

Joining the End of a Round to the Beginning of the Same Round

Chain six, join with a slip stitch in first chain you made to form a ring. Chain three, work 11 double crochet in the ring, insert hook in third chain of beginning chain-three (Figure 56); hook yarn and draw it through the chain and through the loop on the hook; you have now joined the round. Cut yarn and keep this piece as a sample.

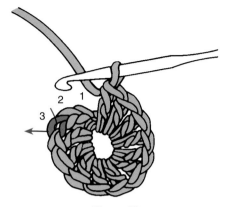

Figure 56

Here is the way the instructions might be written in a pattern:

Rnd 1: Ch 3, 11 dc in ring, join in 3rd ch of beg ch-3.

Lesson 8: Stitch Sampler

Now that you've learned the basic stitches of crochet, the hard part is over!

To help you understand the difference in the way single crochet, half double crochet, double crochet and treble crochet stitches are worked, and the difference in their heights, let's make one more sample.

Chain 17 stitches loosely. Taking care not to work too tightly, single crochet in the second chain from hook and in each of the next three chains; work a half double crochet in each of the next four chains; work a double crochet in each of the next four chains; work a treble crochet in each of the next four chains; fasten off. Your work should look like Photo E.

Photo E

Lesson 9: Working With Colours

Working with colours often involves reading charts, changing colours and learning how to carry or pick up colours.

Working From Charts

Charts are easy to work from once you understand how to follow them. When working from a chart, remember that for each odd-numbered row, you will work the chart from right to left, and for each even-numbered row, you will work the chart from left to right.

Odd-numbered rows are worked on the right side of the piece and even-numbered rows are worked on the wrong side. To help follow across the row, you will find it helpful to place a ruler or sheet of paper directly below the row being worked.

Changing Colours

To change from working colour to a new colour, work the last stitch to be done in the working colour until two loops remain on the hook (Photo F). Draw new colour through the two loops on hook. Drop working colour (Photo G) and continue to work in the new colour. This method can be used when change of colour is at the end of a row or within the row.

Photo F

Carrying or Picking Up Colours

In some patterns, you may need to carry a colour on the wrong side of the work for several stitches or pick up a colour used on the previous row. To carry a colour means to carry the strand on the wrong side of the work. To prevent having loops of unworked yarn, it is helpful to work over the strand of the carried colour. To do this, consider the strand a part of the stitch being worked into and simply insert the hook in the stitch and draw the new colour through (Photo H). When changing from working colour to a colour that has been carried or used on the previous row, always bring this colour under the working colour. This is very important, as it prevents holes in your work.

Photo G

Photo H

Lesson 10: Increasing & Decreasing

Shaping is done by increasing, which adds stitches to make the crocheted piece wider, or decreasing, which subtracts stitches to make the piece narrower.

Tip: Make a practice sample by chaining 15 stitches loosely and working four rows of single crochet with 14 stitches in each row. Do not fasten off at end of last row. Use this sample swatch to practice the following method of increasing stitches.

Increasing

To increase one stitch in single, half double, double or treble crochet, simply work two stitches in one stitch. For example, if you are working in single crochet and you need to increase one stitch, you would work one single crochet in the next stitch; then you would work another single crochet in the same stitch.

For practice: On sample swatch, turn work and chain one. Single crochet in first two stitches; increase in next stitch by working two single crochet in stitch (Figure 57).

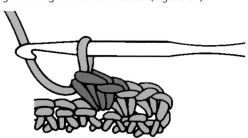

Figure 57
Single Crochet Increase

Repeat increase in each stitch across row to last two stitches; single crochet in each of next two stitches. Count your stitches: You should have 24 stitches. If you don't have 24 stitches, examine your swatch to see if you have increased in each specified stitch. Rework the row if necessary.

Increases in half double, double and treble crochet are shown in Figures 57a, 57b and 57c.

Figure 57a
Half Double Crochet Increase

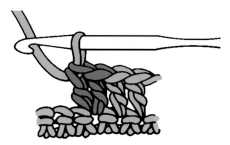

Figure 57b
Double Crochet Increase

Figure 57c
Treble Crochet Increase

Tip: Make another practice sample by chaining 15 loosely and working four rows of single crochet. Do not fasten off at end of last row. Use this sample swatch to practice the following methods of decreasing stitches.

Decreasing

This is how to work a decrease in the four main stitches. Each decrease gives one fewer stitch than you had before.

Single crochet decrease (sc dec): Insert hook and draw up a loop in each of the next two stitches (three loops now on hook), hook yarn and draw through all three loops on the hook (Figure 58).

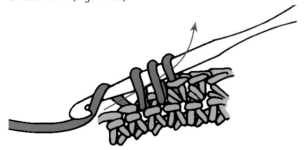

Figure 58

Single crochet decrease made (Figure 59).

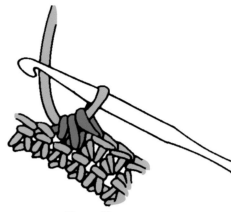

Figure 59

Double crochet decrease (dc dec): Work a double crochet in the specified stitch until two loops remain on the hook (Figure 60).

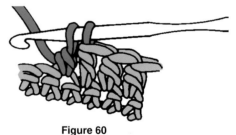

Figure 60

Keeping these two loops on hook, work another double crochet in the next stitch until three loops remain on hook; hook yarn and draw through all three loops on the hook (Figure 61).

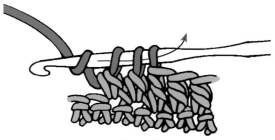

Figure 61

Double crochet decrease made (Figure 62).

Figure 62

Half double crochet decrease (hdc dec): Yo, insert hook in specified stitch and draw up a loop: three loops on the hook (Figure 63).

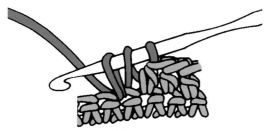

Figure 63

Keeping these three loops on hook, yo and draw up a loop in the next stitch (five loops now on hook), hook yarn and draw through all five loops on the hook (Figure 64).

Figure 64

Half double crochet decrease made (Figure 65).

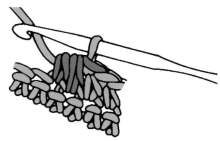

Figure 65

Treble crochet decrease (tr dec): Work a treble crochet in the specified stitch until two loops remain on the hook (Figure 66).

Figure 66

Keeping these two loops on hook, work another treble crochet in the next stitch until 3 loops remain on the hook; hook yarn and draw through all three loops on the hook (Figure 67).

Treble crochet decrease made (Figure 68).

Figure 68

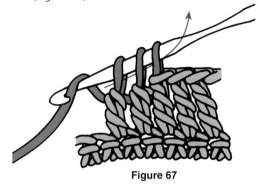

Figure 67

Lesson 11: Joining New Yarn

Never tie or leave knots! In crochet, yarn ends can be easily worked in and hidden because of the density of the stitches. Always leave at least 6 inches when fastening off yarn just used and when joining new yarn. If a flaw or a knot appears in the yarn while you are working from a skein, cut out the imperfection and rejoin the yarn.

Whenever possible, join new yarn at the end of a row. To do this, work the last stitch with the old yarn until two loops remain on the hook, then with the new yarn complete the stitch (Figure 69).

To join new yarn in the middle of a row, when about 12 inches of the old yarn remains, work several more stitches with the old yarn, working the stitches over the end of new yarn (Figure 70 shown in double crochet). Then change yarns in the next stitch as previously explained.

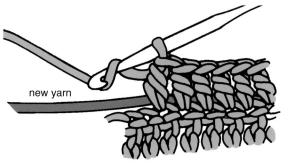

new yarn

Figure 70

Continuing with the new yarn, work the following stitches over the old yarn end.

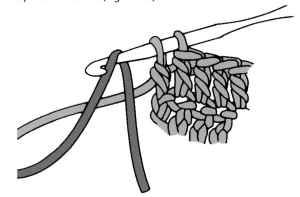

Figure 69

Lesson 12: Finishing & Edging

Finishing

A carefully crocheted project can be disappointing if the finishing is done incorrectly. Correct finishing techniques are not difficult, but they do require time, attention and knowledge of basic techniques.

Weaving in Ends

The first procedure of finishing is to securely weave in all yarn ends. Thread a size 16 steel tapestry needle with yarn end, then weave running stitches either horizontally or vertically on the wrong side of work. First weave about 1 inch in one direction and then ½ inch in the reverse direction. Be sure yarn doesn't show on right side of work. Cut off excess yarn. Never weave in more than one yarn end at a time.

Sewing Seams

In order to avoid bulk, edges in crochet are usually butted together for seaming instead of layered. Do not sew too tightly—seams should be elastic and have the same stretch as the crocheted pieces.

Carefully matching stitches and rows as much as possible, sew the seams with the same yarn you used when crocheting.

Invisible seam: This seam provides a smooth, neat appearance because the edges are woven together invisibly from the right side. Join vertical edges, such as side or sleeve seams, through the matching edge stitches, bringing the yarn up through the posts of the stitches (Figure 71).

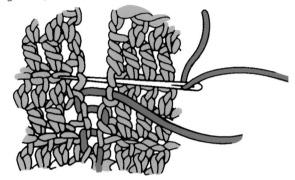

Figure 71

If a firmer seam is desired, weave the edges together through both the tops and the posts of the matching edge stitches.

Backstitch seam: This method gives a strong, firm edge and is used when the seam will have a lot of stress or pull on it. Hold the pieces with right sides together and then sew through both thicknesses as shown (Figure 72).

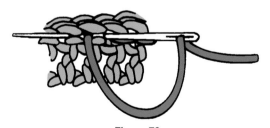

Figure 72

Overcast seam: Strips and pieces of afghans are frequently joined in this manner. Hold the pieces with right sides together and overcast edges, carefully matching stitches on the two pieces (Figure 73).

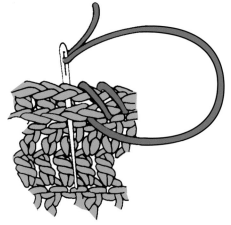

Figure 73

Edges can also be joined in this manner, using only the back loops or the front loops of each stitch (see page 126).

Crocheted Seam: Holding pieces with right sides together, join yarn with a slip stitch at right-side edge. Loosely slip stitch pieces together, being sure not to pull stitches too tightly (Figure 74). You may wish to use a hook one size larger than the one used in the project.

Figure 74

Edging

Single Crochet Edging

A row of single crochet worked around a competed project gives a finished look. The instructions will say to "work a row of single crochet, taking care to keep work flat." This means you need to adjust your stitches as you work. To work the edging, insert hook from front to back through the edge stitch and work a single crochet. Continue evenly along the edge. You may need to skip a row or a stitch here or there to keep the edging from rippling, or add a stitch to keep the work from pulling.

When working around a corner, it is usually necessary to work at least three stitches in the corner centre stitch to keep the corner flat and square (Figure 75).

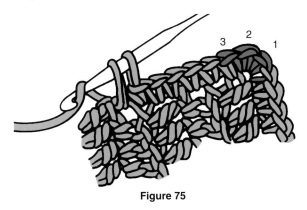

Figure 75

Reverse Single Crochet Edging

A single crochet edging is sometimes worked from left to right for a more dominant edge. To work reverse single crochet, insert hook in stitch to the right (Figure 76), hook yarn and draw through stitch, hook yarn and draw through both loops on the hook (Figure 77).

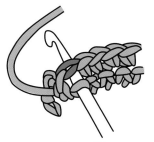

Figure 76

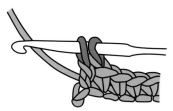

Figure 77

TRIPLE PLAY NECKLACE

Three easy beaded chains give triple the good looks to this eye-catching necklace that will jazz up a variety of summer fashions.

Design | Nazanin S. Fard

Skill Level
EASY

Finished Size

15 inches in length

Materials

Sport weight yarn (124 yds/57g per ball):
    1 ball lilac
Size 0/2.50mm steel crochet hook
81 purple 7 x 9mm crow beads
3-hole spacers: 2
Clasp for closure
Craft glue

2
FINE

First Strand

Row 1: Thread 25 beads on yarn, leaving 6-inch end, ch 2, sc in 2nd ch from hook, **do not turn**. *(1 sc)*

Row 2: Ch 1, sc in sc, do not turn.

Row 3: Pull up bead, ch 1, sc in sc, do not turn.

Next rows: Rep rows 2 and 3 alternately until all beads have been used.

Next rows: Rep row 2 twice. At end of last row, leaving 6-inch end, fasten off.

2nd Strand

Row 1: Thread 27 beads on yarn, leaving 6-inch end, ch 2, sc in 2nd ch from hook, **do not turn**. *(1 sc)*

Next rows: Rep rows 2 to last next rows of First Strand.

3rd Strand

Row 1: Thread 29 beads on yarn, leaving 6-inch end, ch 2, sc in 2nd ch from hook, **do not turn**. *(1 sc)*

Next rows: Rep row 2 to last next rows of First Strand.

Finishing

Working on 1 end, thread each end of each Strand into 1 spacer, being careful to start with First Strand and end with 3rd Strand. Weave in ends, dab with glue to secure.

Thread clasp on yarn, attach yarn to first hole of same spacer, ch 10, pull up clasp, ch 10. Leaving long end, fasten off.

Thread end through the 3rd hole on spacer. Weave in ends and secure with glue.

Rep with strands on other end with rem spacer. ■

Triple Play Necklace
Sample project was crocheted with Aunt Lydia's "Shimmer" Fashion (64 per cent cotton/36 per cent rayon) from Coats & Clark.

Crow beads from Fire Mountain Gems and Beads.

FABULOUS FELTED TOTE

This stylish tote will look great on any outing you might take—you can even take along your latest crochet project.

Design | Jewdy Lambert

Skill Level

INTERMEDIATE

Finished Size

Felted: 13 inches tall x 19 inches long x 5¼ inches deep

Materials

Worsted weight yarn (175 yds/99g per skein):
    6 skeins grey and pink tones

4 MEDIUM

Size I/9/5.5mm crochet hook or size needed to obtain gauge

Tapestry needle

Sewing needle

Sewing thread

Stitch markers

Gauge

4 dc sts = 1½ inches; 4 dc rows = 2¾ inches

Notes

Weave in loose ends as work progresses.

Do not join rounds unless otherwise stated.

Bottom & Ends

Row 1: Beg at centre bottom, ch 32, dc in 4th ch from hook *(sk 3 chs count as first dc)*, dc in each rem ch across, turn. *(30 dc)*

Row 2: Ch 3 *(counts as first dc)*, dc in each dc across, turn.

Rows 3–104: Rep row 2. At end of row 104, fasten off.

First Side

Note: For Tote corners, place first st marker in side edge of row 36 of Bottom & Ends section and 2nd st marker in side edge of row 69 of Bottom & Ends section.

Row 1: Attach yarn in first corner, ch 3, 2 dc in same st, 3 dc in side edge of each row, ending with last 3 in side edge of 2nd corner *(34 sts across bottom)*, turn. *(102 dc)*

Row 2: Ch 3, dc in each dc across, turn.

Rows 3–35: Rep row 2. At the end of row 35, fasten off.

2nd Side

Rows 1–35: Rep rows 1 to 35 on opposite edge of Tote.

Pocket

Row 1: Ch 62, dc in 4th ch from hook, dc in each rem ch across, turn. *(60 dc)*

Rows 2–20: Ch 3, dc in each dc across, turn. At the end of row 20, fasten off.

Handle

Rnd 1: Ch 3, join with sl st to form a ring, 7 dc in ring, **do not join** *(see Notes)*, use st marker to mark rnds. *(7 dc)*

Rnd 2: Dc in each of next 7 dc.

Rep rnd 2 until Handle measures 80 inches from beg, sl st in next dc, fasten off.

Fabulous Felted Tote
Sample project was crocheted with Peruvia Colors (100 per cent Peruvian Highland Wool) from Berroco.

Assembly

Holding First Side and End tog, working through both thicknesses, sl st in each st across edge. Rep sl st on opposite First Side and End.

Holding 2nd Side and End tog, rep sl st across each edge.

With sewing needle and doubled sewing thread, sew Pocket centred on inside edge 7 rows below top edge of First Side.

Handle is woven through 4th row of dc down from top edge. Beg at joined edge of Side and End, *weave from outside in and under 2 sts and back to outside, [weave over 10 dc, weave under 10 dc] twice, with Handle at inside, tie an overhand knot in Handle at the point of Handle on inside edge; leaving approximately 18 inches, tie another overhand knot, sk approximately 23 sts, pass Handle to outside, [weave over 10 dc, weave under 10 dc] twice, pass under 2 dc sts at corner, sk over sts of End, rep from * around. Sew beg and end of tie tog. After felting, the overhand knots will be adjustable.

If, after felting, handle is too long, adjust and tie each section in a knot at each End.

Felting

Place crocheted piece in washer with hot water and a small amount of detergent, wash in a normal cycle. Sometimes two wash cycles are necessary to make a dense fabric. While wet, shape over large shoebox or anything that will maintain Tote shape until dry. ■

EASY TIE WRAP

Add this classy wrap to any outfit, and you are sure to add flair to your night out.

Design | Darla Sims

Skill Level

EASY

Finished Size
17 x 71 inches

Materials
Worsted weight yarn (210 yds/100g per ball):
    4 balls purple

4 MEDIUM

Sizes G/6/4mm and H/8/5mm crochet hooks or
   size needed to obtain gauge
Tapestry needle

Gauge
With H hook: 4 dc = 1 inch

Notes
Weave in ends as work progresses.

Join rounds with a slip stitch unless otherwise stated.

Chain-3 at beginning of double crochet row counts as first double crochet unless otherwise stated.

Special Stitch
Shell: (Dc, ch 3, 3 dc around **post**—*see Stitch Guide on page 126*—of dc just made) in indicated st.

First Half
Row 1: With H hook, ch 4, 2 dc in 4th ch from hook *(beg 3 sk chs count as a dc)*, turn. *(3 dc)*

Row 2: Ch 3 *(see Notes)*, dc in first dc, dc in next dc, 2 dc in 3rd ch of beg 3 sk chs, turn. *(5 dc)*

Row 3: Ch 3, dc in first dc, dc in each of next 3 dc, 2 dc in 3rd ch of beg ch-3, turn. *(7 dc)*

Row 4: Ch 3, dc in each dc and in 3rd ch of beg ch-3, turn.

Row 5: Ch 3, dc in first dc, dc in each of next 5 dc, 2 dc in 3rd ch of beg ch-3, turn. *(9 dc)*

Rows 6 & 7: Rep row 4.

Row 8: Ch 2, dc in next dc, dc in each of next 5 dc, **dc dec** *(see Stitch Guide on page 126)* in next dc and in 3rd ch of beg ch-3, turn. *(7 dc)*

Row 9: Ch 2, dc in each of next 4 dc, dc dec in next dc and in 3rd ch of beg ch-3, turn. *(5 dc)*

Row 10: Ch 2, dc in next dc, dc dec in next dc and in 3rd ch of beg ch-3, turn. *(3 dc)*

Rows 11–13: Rep row 4.

Row 14: Ch 3, 2 dc in first dc, 3 dc in each dc and in 3rd ch of beg ch-3, turn. *(9 dc)*

Row 15: Rep row 4.

Row 16: Ch 3, 2 dc in first dc, 3 dc in each dc and in 3rd ch of beg ch-3, turn. *(27 dc)*

Row 17: Ch 3, 2 dc in each dc to last dc, dc in last dc and in 3rd ch of beg ch-3, turn. *(51 dc)*

Row 18: Ch 3, dc in each of next 2 dc, *sk next 2 dc, **shell** *(see Special Stitch on page 51)* in next dc, sk next 2 dc, dc in each of next 3 dc, rep from * 4 times, shell in next dc, sk next 2 dc, dc in each of next 2 dc and in 3rd ch of beg ch-3, turn. *(6 shells)*

Rows 19–53: Ch 3, dc in each of next 2 dc, *shell in next ch-3 sp, dc in each of next 3 dc, rep from * to last ch-3 sp, shell in last ch-3 sp, dc in each of next 2 dc and in 3rd ch of beg ch-3, turn. At end of last row, fasten off.

2nd Half

Rows 1–52: Rep rows 1 to 52 of First Half. At end of last row, fasten off, leaving 24-inch end for sewing.

Assembly

Hold pieces facing with last row worked held tog at top, with tapestry needle and 24-inch end, sew pieces through **back lps** *(see Stitch Guide on page 126)* only across last row.

Edging

Rnd 1 (RS): With G hook, join in unused lp of beg ch at tip of 1 piece, ch 1, 3 sc in same sp, sc evenly sp around outer edge, working 3 sc in unused lp of beg ch a tip of 2nd piece, join in first sc.

Rnd 2: Ch 1, sc in same sc as joining, ch 5, sc in next sc, ch 5, rep from * around, join in first sc, fasten off. ■

Easy Tie Wrap

Sample project was crocheted with Patons Decor (75 per cent acrylic/ 25 per cent wool) from Spinrite.

CLASSIC IN COPPER HAT & SCARF

Snuggle up in this cute scarf and hat set that's sure to warm up any cold day.

Design | Shelia Leslie

Skill Level

EASY

Size
Adult

Finished Measurements
Hat: 18-inch circumference
Scarf: 3 x 33 inches, excluding Tassels

Materials
Worsted weight yarn (310 yds/100g per ball):
    2 balls persimmon
Size K/10½/6.5mm crochet hook or size needed
    to obtain gauge
Yarn needle
Stitch marker
Pencil

Gauge
With 2 strands yarn held tog: 5 sc = 1½ inches;
    5 sc rows = 1½ inches

Notes
Weave in loose ends as work progresses.

Do not join rounds unless otherwise stated.

Mark first stitch of each round.

Hat

Crown
Rnd 1: Starting at top, with 2 strands held tog, ch 2, 6 sc in 2nd ch from hook, **do not join** *(see Notes)*, **place st marker** *(see Notes)*. *(6 sc)*

Rnd 2: 2 sc in each sc around. *(12 sc)*

Rnd 3: [Sc in next sc, 2 sc in next sc] around. *(18 sc)*

Rnd 4: [Sc in each of next 2 sc, 2 sc in next sc] around. *(24 sc)*

Rnd 5: [2 sc in next sc, sc in each of next 3 sc] around. *(30 sc)*

Rnd 6: [Sc in each of next 4 sc, 2 sc in next sc] around. *(36 sc)*

Rnd 7: [Sc in each of next 5 sc, 2 sc in next sc] around. *(42 sc)*

Rnd 8: [2 sc in next st, sc in each of next 6 sc] around. *(48 sc)*

Rnd 9: [Sc in each of next 7 sc, 2 sc in next sc] around. *(54 sc)*

Rnds 10–20: Sc in each sc around.

Classic in Copper Hat & Scarf
Sample project was crocheted with Red
Heart Symphony (100 per cent acrylic)
from Coats & Clark.

Rnd 21: Sl st in next st, ch 1, sc in same st, ch 2, sk next 2 sts, [sc in next sc, ch 2, sk next 2 sc] around, sl st to join in beg sc. *(18 ch-2 sps)*

Rnd 22: Ch 1, sc in same sc as beg ch-1, 2 sc in next ch-2 sp, [sc in next sc, 2 sc in next ch-2 sp] around, sl st to join in beg sc. *(54 sc)*

Rnd 23: Ch 1, sc in each sc around, sl st to join in beg sc.

Rnd 24: Ch 1, sc in each of next 53 sc, 2 sc in next sc, sl st to join in beg sc. *(55 sc)*

Rnd 25: Ch 2 *(counts as first hdc)*, hdc in same st, 2 hdc in each of next 3 sc, hdc in next sc, [2 hdc in each of next 4 sc, hdc in next sc] around, sl st to join in 2nd ch of beg ch-2. *(99 hdc)*

Rnds 26 & 27: Ch 2, hdc in each hdc around, sl st to join in 2nd ch of beg ch-2.

Rnd 28: Ch 1, **reverse sc** *(Figure 1)* in each st around, sl st to join in beg sc, fasten off.

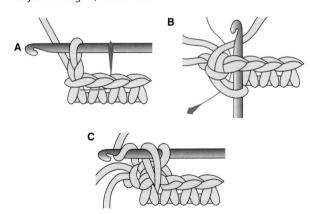

Figure 1
Reverse Single Crochet

Tie

With 2 strands of yarn held tog, ch 110, fasten off.

Weave through ch-2 sps of rnd 21 of Hat. Tie ends in a bow.

Scarf

Row 1: With 2 strands of yarn held tog, ch 3, sc in 2nd ch from hook, sc in next ch, turn. *(2 sc)*

Row 2: Ch 1, 2 sc in each sc across, turn. *(4 sc)*

Row 3: Ch 1, sc in each sc across, turn.

Row 4: Ch 1, 2 sc in first sc, sc in each sc across to last sc, 2 sc in last sc, turn. *(6 sc)*

Row 5: Rep row 3.

Row 6: Rep row 4. *(8 sc)*

Rows 7–17: Rep row 3.

First Half Keyhole

Row 18: Ch 1, sc in each of next 4 sc, turn.

Rows 19–27: Rep row 3. At the end of row 27, fasten off.

2nd Half Keyhole

Row 18: Attach 2 strands of yarn in next unworked st of row 18, ch 1, sc in same st as beg ch-1, sc in each of next 3 sts, turn. *(4 sc)*

Rows 19–27: Rep rows 19 to 27 of First Half Keyhole.

Row 28: With WS facing, attach 2 strands yarn in first sc, ch 1, sc in same sc as beg ch-1, sc in each of next 3 sc and next 4 sc of opposite edge of Keyhole, turn. *(8 sc)*

Rows 29–97: Rep row 3.

Row 98: Ch 1, **sc dec** *(see Stitch Guide on page 126)* in next 2 sc, sc in each of next 4 sc, sc dec in next 2 sc, turn. *(6 sc)*

Row 99: Rep row 3.

Row 100: Ch 1, sc dec in next 2 sc, sc in each of next 2 sc, sc dec in next 2 sc, turn. *(4 sc)*

Row 101: Rep row 3.

Row 102: Ch 1, [sc dec in next 2 sc] twice, fasten off.

Edging

Rnd 1: Working in ends of rows, attach 2 strands of yarn in end of row 102, ch 1, sc in same row as beg ch-1, sc in side edge of each row, at row 1, ch 2, sk opposite side of foundation ch, sc in side edge of row 1 on opposite edge, sc in end of each of next 101 rows, ch 2, sl st to join in first sc, fasten off.

Tassel
Make 2

Cut 2 strands of yarn each 12 inches long and set aside.

Holding 2 strands yarn tog, wrap around 3 spread fingers 16 times. Insert a 12-inch length around centre of bundle and tie in a tight knot at top. Cut through lps at bottom edge. At fold, insert pencil between strands of yarn just below knotted section, smooth strands and tie 2nd 12-inch length directly below pencil, remove pencil. Trim ends even. Sew Tassel to the ch-2 sp at end of Scarf. ∎

FRINGED SHELL SKIRT

Silky bamboo yarn provides the beautiful drape and sassy swing in this flattering skirt with smooth A-line styling.

Design | Jill Hanratty

Skill Level

■■□□ **EASY**

Sizes

Instructions given fit woman's size small; changes for medium, large, X-large, 2X-large, 3X-large and 4X-large are in [ ].

Finished Measurements

Waist: 27 inches *(small)* [30 inches *(medium)*, 33 inches *(large)*, 36 inches *(X-large)*, 39 inches *(2X-large)*, 44 inches *(3X-large)*, 49 inches *(4X-large)*]

Length: 37 inches long for all sizes

Materials

Worsted weight yarn (120 yds/100g per ball):
    8 [9, 10, 11, 12, 13, 15] balls light blue/
    yellow variegated

4 MEDIUM

Size H/8/5mm crochet hook or size needed to
    obtain gauge
Tapestry needle

Gauge

4 dc = 1 inch; 5 dc rows = 3 inches
Each 2-dc shell on waistband = ¾ inches
Take time to check gauge.

Note

Simple length adjustments can be made by adding or omitting rounds between rounds 14 and 20 in pattern.

Special Stitches

2-double crochet shell (2-dc shell): (2 dc, ch 2, 2 dc) in place indicated.

3-double crochet shell (3-dc shell): (3 dc, ch 3, 3 dc) in place indicated.

Small treble shell (small tr shell): (3 tr, ch 3, 3 tr) in place indicated.

Medium treble shell (medium tr shell): (4 tr, ch 4, 4 tr) in place indicated.

Large treble shell (large tr shell): (4 tr, ch 5, 4 tr) in place indicated.

Extra-large treble shell (X-large tr shell): (5 tr, ch 5, 5 tr) in place indicated.

Waistband

Ch 3, (dc, ch 2, 2 dc) in first ch, [ch 1, turn, sk first dc, sl st in next dc and ch sp, **2-dc shell** *(see Special Stitches)* in same ch sp] 30 [33, 36, 39, 42, 48, 54] times, turn. Waistband should measure 22½ [24¾, 27, 29½, 31½, 36, 40½] inches before blocking.

Fringed Shell Skirt
Sample project was crocheted
with Twize (100 per cent bamboo)
from South West Trading Co.

Yoke

Row 1: Working in ends of rows, ch 1, 3 sc in end of each row across, turn. *(90 [99, 108, 117, 126, 144, 162] sc)*

Rnd 2: Now working in rnds, ch 3 *(counts as first dc)*, dc in each st around, join with sl st in 3rd ch of beg ch-3, turn.

Rnd 3: Ch 3, dc in each of next 7 sts, 2 dc in next st, [dc in each of next 8 sts, 2 dc in next st] around, join with sl st in 3rd ch of beg ch-3, turn. *(100 [110, 120, 130, 140, 160, 180] dc)*

Rnd 4: Ch 3, dc in each st around, join with sl st in 3rd ch of beg ch-3, turn.

Rnd 5: Ch 3, dc in each of next 3 sts, 2 dc in next st, [dc in each of next 4 sts, 2 dc in next st] around, join with sl st in 3rd ch of beg ch-3, turn. *(120 [132, 144, 156, 168, 192, 216] dc)*

Rnds 6 & 7: Rep rnd 4.

Rnd 8: Rep rnd 4, **do not turn.**

Body

Rnd 1: Ch 3, *sk next 2 sts, 2-dc shell in next st, sk next 2 sts**, dc in next st, rep from * around, ending last rep at **, join with sl st in 3rd ch of beg ch-3. *(20 [22, 24, 26, 28, 32, 36] 2-dc shells)*

Rnd 2: Ch 3, *2-dc shell in ch sp of next 2-dc shell, sk next 2 dc of shell**, dc in next st, rep from * around, ending last rep at **, join with sl st in 3rd ch of beg ch-3.

Rnd 3: Ch 3, *3-dc shell *(see Special Stitches on page 58)* in ch sp of next 2-dc shell, sk next 2 dc of shell**, dc in next st, rep from * around, ending last rep at **, join with sl st in 3rd ch of beg ch-3.

Rnd 4: Ch 3, *3-dc shell in ch sp of next 3-dc shell, sk next 3 dc of shell**, dc in next st, rep from * around, ending last rep at **, join with sl st in 3rd ch of beg ch-3.

Rnd 5: Ch 3, *small tr shell *(see Special Stitches on page 58)* in ch sp of next 3-dc shell, sk next 3 dc of shell**, dc in next st, rep from * around, ending last rep at **, join with sl st in 3rd ch of beg ch-3.

Rnds 6–12: Ch 3, *small tr shell in ch sp of next small tr shell, sk next 3 tr of shell**, dc in next st, rep from * around, ending last rep at **, join with sl st in 3rd ch of beg ch-3.

Rnd 13: Ch 3, *medium tr shell *(see Special Stitches on page 58)* in ch sp of next small tr shell, sk next 3 tr of shell**, dc in next st, rep from * around, ending last rep at **, join with sl st in 3rd ch of beg ch-3.

Rnds 14–20: Ch 3, *medium tr shell in ch sp of next medium tr shell, sk next 4 tr of shell**, dc in next st, rep from * around, ending last rep at **, join with sl st in 3rd ch of beg ch-3.

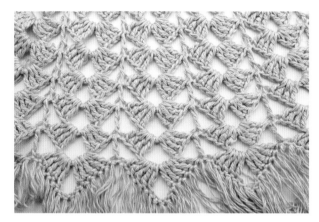

Rnd 21: Ch 3, *large tr shell (see Special Stitches on page 58)* in ch sp of next medium tr shell, sk next 4 tr of shell**, dc in next st, rep from * around, ending last rep at **, join with sl st in 3rd ch of beg ch-3.

Rnd 22: Ch 3, *X-large tr shell (see Special Stitches on page 58)* in ch sp of next large tr shell, sk next 4 tr of shell**, dc in next st, rep from * around, ending last rep at **, join with sl st in 3rd ch of beg ch-3. Fasten off.

Block to finished garment measurement.

Drawstring

Holding 2 strands of yarn tog, leaving 16-inch end, ch 180 [200, 220, 240, 260, 290, 330]. Fasten off.

Beg at open end of Waistband, weave Drawstring through ch sps.

Tassel
Make 2

Cut 40 strands each 16 inches long. Tie separate strand around centre of all strands held tog, fold in half. Wrap separate strand several times around all strands 1 inch below fold. Secure ends. Trim ends.

Attach 1 Tassel to each end of Drawstring.

Fringe

Cut 1 strand 7 inches long. Fold strand in half, pull fold through st, pull ends through fold. Pull to tighten.

Fringe in each st around bottom of Body. ∎

EASY SUMMER VEST OR TOP

You can increase your wardrobe twice over by adding this versatile, attractive top.

Design | Darla Sims

Skill Level

EASY

Sizes

Instructions given fit 32–34-inch bust *(small)*; changes for 36–38-inch bust *(medium)*, 40–42-inch bust *(large)*, 44–46-inch bust *(X-large)*, 48–50-inch bust *(2X-large)*, 52–54-inch bust *(3X-large)*, 56–58-inch bust *(4X-large)* and 60–62-inch bust *(5X-large)* are in [ ].

Finished Measurements

Bust: 36 inches *(small)* [40 inches *(medium)*, 44 inches *(large)*, 48 inches *(X-large)*, 52 inches *(2X-large)*, 56 inches *(3X-large)*, 60 inches *(4X-large)*, 64 inches *(5X-large)*]]

Materials

Worsted weight yarn (400 yds per ball):
    2 [2, 3, 4, 4, 5, 5, 6] balls cranberry
Sizes F/5/3.75mm, G/6/4mm and H/8/5mm
    crochet hooks or size needed to obtain gauge
Tapestry needle
Stitch markers

Gauge

Size H hook: 3 dc = 1 inch

Notes

Weave in loose ends as work progresses.

Join rounds with a slip stitch unless otherwise stated.

Top is made of 2 pieces worked vertically. Each piece is folded in half horizontally *(short ends together)* to create 1 half of garment, going up and over shoulders from lower edge of front to lower edge of back. Pieces are joined at centre front and back to create V-neck openings.

Front & Back
Make 2

Row 1: With size H hook, ch 122 [126, 126, 126, 128, 128, 132, 132], dc in 4th ch from hook *(beg 3 chs count as first dc)*, dc in each rem ch across, turn. *(120 [124, 124, 126, 126, 130, 130] dc)*

Row 2: Ch 3 *(counts as first dc)*, dc in each dc across, turn.

Rep row 2 until piece measures 9 [10, 11, 12, 13, 14, 15, 16] inches wide, fasten off.

Assembly
Fold each piece in half *(see Notes)* and place st marker at both ends of fold to mark shoulder line *(fold line)*. For all sizes, measure 8 inches down from shoulder line on both pieces for front neck opening. Place pieces side by side. Beg at lower front and working through **back lps** *(see Stitch Guide on page 126)* only, sew pieces tog to st

Easy Summer Vest or Top
Sample project was crocheted with Aunt Lydia's Quick Crochet (75 per cent cotton/ 25 per cent acrylic) from Coats & Clark.

markers. For all sizes, place markers 6 inches down from shoulder line on both pieces for back neck opening. Beg at lower edge, sew pieces tog to st markers in same manner as for front neck opening.

For armholes, measure and place st markers 8 [8½, 8½, 8½, 9, 9, 9½, 10] inches down from shoulder line on front and back outer edge of each piece. Working through back lps only, sew side seams from lower edge to st markers.

Neck Edging

Rnd 1 (RS): With size G hook, attach yarn with sc in 1 shoulder st marker, ch 1, working in sts down neck edge, work 25 sc evenly sp from shoulder to 1 st before bottom of V-neck, **sc dec** *(see Stitch Guide on page 126)* in next st and in next st on opposite neck edge, work 25 sc evenly sp up to next shoulder st marker, working on back neck edge, work 18 sc evenly sp down to 1 st before bottom of V-neck, sc dec in next st and in next st on opposite neck edge, work 18 sc evenly sp up to first sc, join in beg sc, fasten off. *(88 sc)*

Armhole Edging
Make 2

Rnd 1 (RS): With size F hook, attach yarn in bottom of armhole opening, ch 1, working in ends of rows around armhole opening, work 25 [27, 27, 27, 29, 29, 31, 33] sc evenly sp up to shoulder and work 25 [27, 27, 27, 29, 29, 31, 33] sc evenly sp from shoulder down to underarm on opposite edge, join in beg sc. *(50 [54, 54, 54, 58, 62, 66] sc)*

Rnd 2: Ch 1, sc in same sc as beg ch-1, sc in each rem sc around, join in beg sc.

Rnd 3: Rep rnd 2, fasten off.

Lower Edging

Rnd 1 (RS): With size F hook, attach yarn in right-hand side seam, working in end sts of dc rows, ch 1, work 30 [32, 34, 36, 38, 40, 42, 44] sc evenly sp to centre front and another 30 [32, 34, 36, 38, 40, 42, 44] sc evenly sp to left-hand side seam, work 30 [32, 34, 36, 38, 40, 42, 44] sc evenly sp to centre back and 30 [32, 34, 36, 38, 40, 42, 44] sc evenly sp to right-hand side seam, join in beg sc. *(120 [128, 136, 144, 152, 160, 168, 176] sc)*

Rnd 2: Ch 1, sc in same sc as beg ch-1, sc in next sc, sc dec in next 2 sc, [sc in each of next 2 sc, sc dec in next 2 sc] around, join in beg sc. *(90 [96, 102, 108, 114, 120, 126, 132] sc)*

Rnd 3: Ch 1, sc in same sc as beg ch-1, sc in each rem sc around, join in beg sc.

Rnds 4 & 5: Rep rnd 3. At the end of rnd 5, fasten off. ∎

SPA SET

Treat yourself to a day at the spa with these pretty bath accessories.

Design | Elaine Bartlett

Skill Level
EASY

Finished Sizes
Washcloth: 8½ x 8¼ inches
Scrubbie Washcloth: 7½ inches square
Back Scrubbie: 3 x 18½, excluding Handles
Soap Sachet: 3½ x 6 inches

Materials
Worsted weight yarn (87 yds/50g per ball):
    3 balls light green
Size H/8/5mm crochet hook or size needed to
    obtain gauge
Tapestry needle
Large-eyed tapestry needle
Stitch marker
Mesh sponge in desired colour

Gauge
14 sc = 4 inches; 20 sc rows = 4 inches

Notes
Weave in loose ends as work progresses.

Join rounds with a slip stitch unless otherwise stated.

Washcloth
Row 1 (WS): Ch 29, sc in 2nd ch from hook, sc in each rem ch across, turn. *(28 sc)*

Rows 2–38: Ch 1, sc in each sc across, turn.

Row 39: Ch 1, sc in each sc across, **do not turn.**

Rnd 40: Now working in rnds, ch 1, work 24 sc across side edge of Washcloth, ending with (sc, ch 2, sc) in corner st, sc in each ch across opposite side of foundation ch, work (sc, ch 2, sc) in corner st, work 24 sc across side edge of Washcloth, (sc, ch 2, sc) in corner st, sc in each sc across row 39, (sc, ch 2, sc) in corner st, join in first sc.

Rnd 41: Ch 1, sc in each sc around, working 3 sc in each corner ch-2 sp, join in beg sc, fasten off.

Scrubbie Washcloth
Rnd 1 (RS): Starting at centre, ch 4, join in first ch to form a ring, ch 2 *(counts as first dc)*, 2 dc in ring, ch 2, [3 dc in ring, ch 2] 3 times, join in 3rd ch of ch-3. *(12 dc, 4 ch-2 sps)*

Rnd 2: Ch 2, dc in each of next 2 dc, *(2 dc, ch 2, 2 dc) in corner ch-2 sp **, dc in each of next 3 dc, rep from * around, ending last rep at **, join in 2nd ch of ch-2. *(28 dc, 4 ch-2 sps)*

Rnd 3: Ch 2, dc in each dc around, working (2 dc, ch 2, 2 dc) in each corner ch-2 sp, join in 2nd ch of ch-2. *(44 dc, 4 ch-2 sps)*

Rnd 4: Ch 2, dc in each dc around, working (dc, ch 2, dc) in each corner ch-2 sp, join in 2nd ch of ch-2. *(52 dc, 4 ch-2 sps)*

Spa Set

Sample projects were crocheted with
Bernat Organic Cotton (100 per cent
organic cotton) from Spinrite.

Thread rem 2-inch lengths onto large-eyed tapestry needle. Pass needle through centre of mesh from RS to WS of Washcloth. Remove 1 length from needle, pass needle back through to RS of Washcloth slightly left of centre, remove rem length from needle. Thread length on WS of Washcloth onto needle and pass needle back through to RS of Washcloth slightly left of centre, knot ends to secure and weave each rem end into Washcloth.

Back Scrubbie

Row 1 (WS): Ch 10, sc in 2nd ch from hook, sc in each rem ch across, turn. *(9 sc)*

Row 2: Ch 1, sc in each sc across, turn.

Rows 3–5: Rep row 2.

Row 6: Ch 1, sc in each of next 2 sc, [tr in next sc, sc in next sc] 3 times, sc in last sc, turn. *(6 sc, 3 tr)*

Row 7: Rep row 2.

Row 8: Ch 1, sc in each of next 3 sc, [tr in next sc, sc in next sc] twice, sc in each of next 2 sc, turn. *(7 sc, 2 tr)*

Row 9: Rep row 2.

Rows 10–69: [Rep rows 6 to 9 consecutively] 15 times.

Row 70: Rep row 6.

Rows 71–76: Rep row 2.

Rnd 77: Now working in rnds, work 2 more sc in same st as last sc of row 76 *(3 sc in corner)*, working in ends of rows, work 1 sc in each row across, ending with 3 sc in first ch of opposite side of foundation ch, sc in each of next 7 chs, 3 sc in last ch, sc in side edge of each row, ending with 2 sc in same sc as first sc of row 76, join in first sc of row 76.

Rnd 5: Rep rnd 3. *(68 dc, 4 ch-2 sps)*

Rnd 6: Rep rnd 4. *(76 dc, 4 ch-2 sps)*

Rnd 7: Rep rnd 3. *(92 dc, 4 ch-2 sps)*

Rnd 8: Ch 1, sc in same st as beg ch-1, sc in each dc around, working 3 sc in each corner ch-2 sp, join in beg sc, fasten off. *(104 sc)*

Assembly

Prepare mesh sponge by cutting the tie that holds the sponge tog. Cut the mesh sponge in half. Using a 24-inch length of yarn, gather half of the mesh tog and tie yarn around the middle of the mesh and knot securely, leaving 2-inch lengths of yarn, fasten off.

Rnd 78: Sl st in each st around to middle st of last corner *(before joining)*, ch 20 *(for first Handle)*, using care not to twist ch, sl st in middle st of next corner, turn, sl st in back bump of each ch of ch-20, fasten off. Attach yarn in centre st of next corner 3-sc group, ch 20 *(for 2nd Handle)*, taking care not to twist ch, sl st in back bump of each ch of ch-20, fasten off.

Soap Sachet

Body
Make 2

Row 1 (RS): Ch 12, sc in 2nd ch from hook, sc in each rem ch across, turn. *(11 sc)*

Rows 2–24: Ch 1, sc in each sc across, turn. At the end of row 24, fasten off.

Assembly
Rnd 1: Holding Body pieces tog matching rows and working through both thicknesses, attach yarn in side edge of row 24, ch 1, sc in same st as beg ch-1 *(RS row)*, [sk next WS row, sc in next row] across, working across opposite side of foundation ch, 3 sc in corner, sc in each ch across to last ch, 3 sc in last ch, working up side edge of rows, sc in side edge of row 1, [sk next WS row, sc in next row] across edge, **do not fasten off**.

Top Edging
Rnd 1: Ch 1, sc evenly sp around top opening, join in beg sc.

Rnd 2: Ch 3 *(counts as first dc)*, dc in each sc around, join in 3rd ch of beg ch-3.

Rnd 3: Ch 1, sc in same st as beg ch-1, sc in each dc around, join, fasten off.

Tie
Leaving a 6-inch length at beg, ch 50 tightly, leaving a 6-inch length, fasten off.

Starting at centre front of Soap Sachet, weave Tie through sps between dc sts of rnd 2 of Top Edging, knot ends tog, trim each end to approximately 1 inch. ∎

WARM & SPICY!

*This spicy set would look equally
as good in two solid colours
such as burgundy and cream.*

Design | Laura Gebhardt

Skill Level
INTERMEDIATE

Finished Sizes
Scarf: 5¼ x 64 inches, excluding Fringe
Hat: Fits adult

Materials
Worsted weight yarn (solid: 7 oz/364 yds/198g;
    multi: 5 oz/255 yds/141g per skein):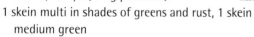
        1 skein multi in shades of greens and rust, 1 skein
            medium green
Size H/8/5mm crochet hook or size needed to obtain
    gauge
Yarn needle
Stitch marker

Gauge
8 groups of hdc dec = 5 inches; 6 rows = 3 inches; 4 sc =
    1 inch; 4 rnds = 1 inch

Notes
Weave in loose ends as work progresses.

Join rounds with a slip stitch unless otherwise stated.

Special Stitch
Half double crochet decrease (hdc dec): Yo, insert hook
in next st, yo, draw up lp, yo, draw up a lp in next st, yo,
draw through all 5 lps on hook.

Scarf

Body
Row 1: With medium green, leaving an 8-inch length at
beg, ch 211, **hdc dec** *(see Special Stitch)* in 3rd and 4th
chs from hook, [ch 1, hdc dec in next 2 chs] across to last
ch, ch 1, hdc in last ch, leaving an 8-inch length, fasten
off, turn. *(1 hdc, 104 dec groups, 1 hdc)*

Row 2: Leaving an 8-inch length at beg, draw up lp of
multi in shades of greens and rust in top of last hdc of
previous row, ch 2 *(counts as first hdc)*, hdc dec in next
2 ch-1 sps, [ch 1, working in same ch-1 sp as 2nd half of
previous dec and next ch-1 sp, work hdc dec] across to
last hdc, ch 1, hdc in end ch, leaving an 8-inch length of
yarn, fasten off, turn.

Row 3: With medium green, rep row 2.

Rows 4–11: [Rep rows 2 and 3 alternately] 4 times.

Fringe
Cut 14 17-inch strands each of medium green and multi
in shades of greens and rust. Holding 1 strand of each
colour tog, incorporating a beg or ending 8-inch length
into each Fringe, fold strands in half, insert hook in end of
row, draw strands through at fold to form a lp on hook,
draw all strands through lp on hook. Trim ends evenly.

Warm & Spicy
Sample project was crocheted with
Red Heart Super Saver (100 per cent
acrylic) from Coats & Clark.

Hat

Crown

Rnd 1: Beg at top of hat with medium green, ch 2, 6 sc in 2nd ch from hook, **do not join**, use st marker to mark rnds. *(6 sc)*

Rnd 2: 2 sc in each sc around. *(12 sc)*

Rnd 3: [Sc in next sc, 2 sc in next sc] around. *(18 sc)*

Rnd 4: [Sc in each of next 2 sc, 2 sc in next sc] around. *(24 sc)*

Rnd 5: Sc in each sc around.

Rnd 6: Rep rnd 4. *(32 sc)*

Rnd 7: [Sc in each of next 3 sc, 2 sc in next sc] around. *(40 sc)*

Rnd 8: Rep rnd 5.

Rnd 9: [Sc in each of next 4 sc, 2 sc in next sc] around. *(48 sc)*

Rnd 10: Rep rnd 5.

Rnd 11: Rep rnd 7. *(60 sc)*

Rnd 12: Rep rnd 5.

Rnd 13: Rep rnd 9. *(72 sc)*

Rnds 14 & 15: Rep rnd 5.

Rnd 16: [Sc in each of next 5 sc, 2 sc in next sc] around. *(84 sc)*

Rnds 17–30: Rep rnd 5.

Rnd 31: Working in **front lps** *(see Stitch Guide on page 126)* only, sc in each st around, join in beg sc, drop medium green, attach multi with sl st in first sc, remove st marker.

Cuff

Rnd 32: Ch 1, hdc dec in same st and next sc, ch 1, [hdc dec in next 2 sc, ch 1] around, join in top of first hdc dec, drop multi, draw up a lp of medium green, turn. *(42 dec groups)*

Rnd 33: Ch 1, hdc dec in next 2 ch-1 sps, ch 1, [working in same ch-1 sp as and half of previous dec and next ch-1 sp, work hdc dec, ch 1] around, join in first hdc dec, drop medium green, draw up a lp of multi in shades of greens and rust, turn.

Rnds 34 & 35: Rep rnds 32 and 33.

Rnd 36: Rep rnd 32. At the end of rnd 36 draw up lp of medium green, fasten off multi in shades of greens and rust.

Rnd 37: Ch 1, sc in each hdc dec and each ch-1 sp around, join in first sc, fasten off.

Pompom

Wrap multi around 3 fingers of left hand loosely 75 times. Carefully remove lps from fingers and wrap a 9-inch piece of yarn tightly several times around centre of bundle and knot. Cut through lps at both ends, fluff and trim ends. Attach to top of Hat. ■

BOOKMARKS

This colourful set of four bookmarks will make a great gift for any family member or friend.

Butterfly

Design | Barbara Neid

Skill Level ◼◼◻◻
EASY

Finished Size
2⅝ x 10½ inches, including tassel

Materials
Size 10 crochet cotton:
   5 yds shaded pinks
Size 3/2.10mm steel crochet hook or size needed to obtain gauge
Tapestry needle

Gauge
Gauge not important to this project.

Notes
Weave in ends as work progresses.

Join rounds with a slip stitch unless otherwise stated.

Chain-3 at beginning of double crochet round counts as first double crochet unless otherwise stated.

Body
Rnd 1 (RS): Ch 8, join in first ch to form a ring, **ch 3** *(see Notes)*, 2 dc in ring, ch 3, [3 dc in ring, ch 3] 7 times, **join** *(see Notes)* in 3rd ch of beg ch-3. *(24 dc, 8 ch-3 sps)*

Rnd 2: Sl st in each of next 2 dc, sl st in next ch-3 sp, ch 3, (3 dc, ch 3, 4 dc) in same sp, (4 dc, ch 3, 4 dc) in each rem ch-3 sp around, join in 3rd ch of beg ch-3. *(64 dc, 8 ch-3 sps)*

Rnd 3: Sl st in each of next 3 sts, sl st in next ch-3 sp, ch 3, (4 dc, ch 3, 5 dc) in same sp, sk next 3 dc, sl st in sp between next 2 dc, *(5 dc, ch 3, 5 dc) in next ch-3 sp, sk next 3 dc, sl st in sp between next 2 dc, rep from * around, join in 3rd ch of beg ch-3, fasten off.

Finishing
Fold WS of piece in half matching points to form Butterfly. Wrap 1 end of thread around centre of butterfly 4 times, tie in knot, ch 60 (tail), sl st in 2nd ch from hook, sl st in each rem ch, fasten off.

Tassel
Cut 8 strands each 4 inches long. Holding all strands tog, fold in half, insert hook in last ch of Tail, draw fold through, draw ends through fold, tighten.

Heart

Design | Barbara Neid

Skill Level
EASY

Finished Size
2 x 11½ inches, including tassel

Materials
Size 10 crochet cotton:
   5 yds dark red
Size 3/2.10mm steel crochet hook or size needed to
   obtain gauge
Tapestry needle

Gauge
Gauge not important to this project.

Note
Weave in ends as work progresses.

Heart Centre
Row 1: Ch 11, dc in 5th ch from hook (beg 4 sk chs count as first dc), *ch 1, sk next ch, dc in next ch, rep from * across, turn. *(5 dc)*

Row 2: Ch 4 *(counts as first dc and ch-1 sp)*, sk next ch-1 sp, dc in next dc, *ch 1, sk next ch-1 sp, dc in next dc, rep from * twice, ch 1, dc in 3rd ch of beg 4 sk chs, turn.

Rows 3 & 4: Ch 4, sk next ch-1 sp, dc in next dc, *ch 1, sk next ch-1 sp, dc in next dc, rep from * twice, ch 1, dc in 3rd ch of beg ch-4, turn. At end of last row, **do not turn.**

Heart Top
Row 1: Ch 1, working across next side in sps formed by edge sts, 2 sc in each of first 2 sps, ch 2, 2 sc in each of last 2 sps, turn. *(8 sc)*

Row 2: Ch 1, sc in first sc, sk next 3 sc, 12 dc in next ch-2 sp, sk next 4 sc, sc in next dc on row 4, 2 sc in each of next 2 ch-2 sps on row 4, ch 2, 2 sc in last 2 ch-1 sps on row 4, turn.

Row 3: Ch 1, sc in first sc, sk next 3 sc, 12 dc in next ch-2 sp, sk next 4 sc, sl st in next sc on row 2, **do not turn**, ch 60 *(tail)*, sl st in 2nd ch from hook, sl st in each rem ch across, sl st in same sc on row 2.

Edging
Ch 1, working around outer edge, sc in each st, 2 sc in each ch sp or sp formed by edge dc and 4 sc in tip, join with a sl st in first sc, fasten off.

Tassel
With dark red, work same as Tassel for Butterfly.

Flower

Design | Barbara Neid

Skill Level
EASY

Finished Size
2½ x 11½ inches, including tassel

Materials
Size 10 crochet cotton:
   5 yds golden yellow and green
Size 3/2.10mm steel crochet hook or size needed to
   obtain gauge
Tapestry needle

Gauge
Gauge not important to this project.

Bookmarks

Sample projects were crocheted
with J. & P. Royale Classic Crochet
size 10 crochet cotton (100 per cent
mercerized cotton) from Coats & Clark .

Notes

Weave in ends as work progresses.

Join rounds with a slip stitch unless otherwise stated.

Chain-3 at beginning of double crochet row/round counts as first double crochet unless otherwise stated.

Body

Rnd 1: Starting at centre with golden yellow, ch 6, join in first ch to form a ring, ch 1, 12 sc in ring, **join** *(see Notes)* in **front lp** *(see Stitch Guide on page 126)* of first sc. *(12 sc)*

Rnd 2: Ch 3 *(see Notes)*, sl st in same lp as joining sl st, working in front lps only, (sl st, ch 3, sl st) in each rem sc, join in **back lp** *(see Stitch Guide on page 126)* of joining sl st of rnd 1.

Rnd 3: Working in back lps of sc of rnd 1, *sl st in next st, ch 9, sl st in 2nd ch from hook, sl st in each rem ch *(petal)*, sl st in next sc on rnd 1, rep from * around, join in joining sl st. *(6 petals)*

Rnd 4: Working in chs and in sl sts of petals, *sc in each of next 2 sts, hdc in each of next 2 sts, dc in next st, hdc in next st, sc in next st, sl st in next st, ch 1, working on opposite side of petal, sl st in next st, sc in next st, hdc in next st, dc in next st, hdc in each of next 2 sts, sl st in next 2 sts on rnd 2, rep from * around, join in first sc, fasten off.

Leaf

Row 1: Join green in any st on back of Flower, ch 12, sl st in 2nd ch from hook, sl st in each ch across, turn.

Row 2: Sl st in first st, ch 1, sc in next st, hdc in each of next 3 sts, dc in each of next 3 sts, dc in each of next 2 sts, hdc in each of next 2 sts, sc in next st, 2 sc in last st, working on opposite side of foundation ch, sc in each of first 2 sts, hdc in each of next 2 sts, dc in each of next

2 sts, hdc in each of next 2 sts, dc in each of next 2 sts, hdc in each of next 3 sts, sc in next st, sl st in last st, ch 60 *(tail)*, sl st in 2nd ch from hook, sl st in each ch across, fasten off.

Tassel

With green, work same as Tassel for Butterfly.

Apple

Design | Luella Hinrichsen

Skill Level ◼◼◻◻ EASY

Finished Size

2 inches x 10 inches, including worm

Materials

Size 10 crochet cotton:
    5 yds red
    1 yd each green, tan, gold, white
Size 5/1.90mm steel crochet hook or size needed to obtain gauge
Tapestry needle

Gauge

Gauge not important to this project.

Notes

Weave in ends as work progresses.

Join rounds with a slip stitch unless otherwise stated.

Body

Row 1: With red, ch 3, 2 sc in 2nd ch from hook, 2 sc in last ch, turn. *(4 sc)*

Row 2: Ch 1, sc in each st across, turn.

Row 3: Ch 1, 2 sc in each sc across, turn. *(8 sc)*

Row 4: Rep row 2.

Row 5: Ch 1, 2 sc in first sc, sc in each st across to last sc, 2 sc in last sc, turn. *(10 sc)*

Row 6: Rep row 2.

Row 7: Rep row 5. *(12 sc at end of row)*

Rows 8–10: Rep row 2.

Row 11: Rep row 5. *(14 sc at end of row)*

Row 12: Rep row 2.

Row 13: Ch 1, **sc dec** *(see Stitch Guide on page 126)* in first 2 sc, sc in each sc across to last 2 sc, sc dec in last 2 sc, turn. *(12 sc)*

Row 14: Ch 1, sc dec in first 2 sc, (sc, hdc, sc) in next sc, sc in next sc, sl st in next 4 sc, sc in next sc, (sc, hdc, sc) in next sc, sc dec in last 2 sts, turn. *(14 sts)*

Edging
Ch 1, working around outer edge, sc in each st and in end of each row, **join** *(see Notes)* in first sc, fasten off.

Stem
Join tan in 7th sc of Edging, ch 5, sl st in 2nd ch from hook, sl st in each rem ch across, sl st in next sc of Edging, fasten off.

Leaf
Join green in last sl st on Stem, ch 10, sc in 2nd ch from hook, hdc in next ch, dc in next ch, tr in next ch, dc in next ch, hdc in each of next 2 chs, sc in next ch, sl st in last ch, working in unused lps on opposite of foundation ch, sc in next ch, hdc in each of next 2 chs, dc in next ch, tr in next ch, dc in next ch, hdc in next ch, sc in last ch, join in first sc, fasten off.

Worm
With gold, ch 16, sl st in 2nd ch from hook, sc in each of next 3 chs, 3 sc in next ch, sc in next 4 chs, sk next ch, sc in each of next 2 chs, 3 sc in next ch, sc in each of last ch, fasten off.

Finishing
Join white around **post** *(see Stitch Guide on page 126)* of same sc as first sl st on Stem made, ch to measure 6 inches, join in first sc on Worm, fasten off. ■

GRANNY'S HANGERS

These quick-to-stitch covers for your hangers will be much appreciated.

Design | Kyleigh C. Hawke

Skill Level

EASY

Finished Size

To fit over 16¾-inch wide plastic hanger.

Materials

Worsted weight yarn:

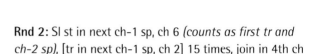

    40 yds A

    30 yds B

    15 yds C

Size H/8/5mm crochet hook or size needed to obtain gauge

Tapestry needle

Gauge

Rnds 1 and 2 = 4 inches across

Notes

Weave in ends as work progresses.

Join rounds with a slip stitch unless otherwise stated.

Chain-3 at beginning of double crochet round counts as first double crochet unless otherwise stated.

Cover

Rnd 1 (RS): With A, ch 8, join in first ch to form a ring, ch 5 *(counts as first tr and ch-1 sp)*, [tr in ring, ch 1] 15 times, **join** *(see Notes)* in 4th ch of beg ch-5. *(16 tr, 16 ch-1 sps)*

Rnd 2: Sl st in next ch-1 sp, ch 6 *(counts as first tr and ch-2 sp)*, [tr in next ch-1 sp, ch 2] 15 times, join in 4th ch of beg ch-6, fasten off. *(16 tr, 16 ch-2 sps)*

Rnd 3: Join B in any ch-2 sp, **ch 3** *(see Notes)*, (3 dc, ch 2, 4 dc) in same sp, ch 1, sc in next ch-2 sp, [ch 3, sc in next ch-2 sp] 6 times, ch 1, (4 dc, ch 2, 4 dc) in next ch-2 sp, ch 1, sc in next ch-2 sp, [ch 3, sc in next ch-2 sp] 6 times, ch 1, join in 3rd ch of beg ch-3. *(12 ch-3 sps, 4 ch-1 sps, 2 ch-2 sps)*

Rnd 4: Sl st in each of next 3 dc, sl st in next ch-2 sp, ch 3, (3 dc, ch 2, 4 dc) in same sp, ch 1, sk next ch-1 sp, [4 dc in next ch-3 sp, ch 1] 6 times, sk next ch-1 sp, (4 dc, ch 2, 4 dc) in next ch-2 sp, ch 1, sk next ch-1 sp, [4 dc in next ch-3 sp, ch 1] 6 times, sk next ch-1 sp, join in 3rd ch of beg ch-3, fasten off. *(14 ch-1 sps, 2 ch-2 sps)*

Rnd 5: Join C in any ch-2 sp, ch 3, (3 dc, ch 2, 4 dc) in same sp, 4 dc in each of next 7 ch-1 sps, (4 dc, ch 2, 4 dc) in next ch-2 sp, 4 dc in each of last 7 ch-1 sps, join in 3rd ch of beg ch-3. *(9 groups of 4-dc between ch-2 sps)*

Rnd 6: Sl st in each of next 3 sts, sl st in next ch-2 sp, ch 3, (3 dc, ch 2, 4 dc) in same sp, 4 dc in sp between each 4-dc group across to next ch-2 sp, (4 dc, ch 2, 4 dc) in ch-2 sp, 4 dc in sp between each 4-dc group across, join in 3rd ch of beg ch-3. *(10 groups of 4-dc between ch-2 sps)*

Granny's Hangers
Sample projects were crocheted with Red Heart Super Saver (100 per cent acrylic) from Coats & Clark.

Rnd 7: Sl st in each of next 3 sts, sl st in next ch-2 sp, ch 3, (3 dc, ch 2, 4 dc) in same sp, ch 1, [sk next 3 dc, 4 dc in sp between next 2 dc, ch 1] 9 times, (4 dc, ch 2, 4 dc) in next ch-2 sp, ch 1, [sk next 3 dc, 4 dc in sp between next 2 dc, ch 1] 9 times, join in 3rd ch of beg ch-3, fasten off. *(10 ch-1 sps between ch-2 sps)*

Rnd 8: Join A in first ch-2 sp, ch 3, 3 dc in same sp, ch 1, [4 dc in next ch-1 sp, ch 1] 10 times, 4 dc in next ch-2 sp, ch 1, [4 dc in next ch-1 sp, ch 1] 10 times, join in 3rd ch of beg ch-3. *(22 ch-1 sps)*

Rnd 9: Sl st in each of next 3 dc, sl st in next ch-1 sp, ch 3, 3 dc in same sp, ch 1, *4 dc in next ch-1 sp, ch 1, rep from * around, join in 3rd ch of beg ch-3, fasten off.

Assembly

Fold piece in half with ch-2 sps at fold. Insert hanger. Matching sts, with A and tapestry needle and working through both thicknesses, sew first 20 dc and 4 ch-1 sps along top edge tog, sk next 4 sts around curved part of hanger, sew last 20 dc and 4 ch-1 sps tog.

Fringe

Cut 12 strands of A each 12 inches long. Hold strands tog and fold in half, insert hook in ring formed on rnd 1, draw fold through, draw ends through fold, tighten. Trim ends. ■

PASTEL SHELLS AFGHAN

Cuddle your precious little one in this pretty pastel blanket that is just the right size.

Design | Katherine Eng

Skill Level

EASY

Finished Size
29 x 40 inches

Materials
DK weight yarn (431 yds/160g per skein):
   1 skein each soft blue, soft mauve, baby
      pink and light yellow
Size I/9/5.5mm crochet hook or size needed to obtain
   gauge
Tapestry needle

Gauge
3 shells and 4 sc = 4 inches; Rows 1–4 = 2½ inches

Notes
Weave in loose ends as work progresses.

Join rounds with a slip stitch unless otherwise stated.

Special Stitches
Small shell: 3 dc in indicated st.

Large shell: 5 dc in indicated st.

Afghan
Row 1 (RS): With soft blue, ch 134, sc in 2nd ch from hook, [sk next ch, **small shell** *(see Special Stitches)* in next ch, sk next ch, sc in next ch] across, turn. *(33 shells)*

Row 2: Ch 3 *(counts as first dc)*, dc in same st as beg ch-3, [sc in centre dc of next small shell, small shell in next sc] across, ending with 2 dc in last sc, turn.

Row 3: Ch 1, sc in first dc, [small shell in next sc, sc in centre dc of next small shell] across, ending with sc in last dc, turn.

Row 4: Rep row 2, fasten off.

Row 5: Attach soft mauve with sl st in first dc, rep row 3.

Row 6: Rep row 2, fasten off.

Row 7: Attach light yellow with sl st in first dc, rep row 3.

Row 8: Rep row 2, fasten off.

Row 9: Attach baby pink with sl st in first dc, rep row 3.

Row 10: Rep row 2, fasten off.

Row 11: Attach soft blue with sl st in first dc, rep row 3.

Rows 12 & 13: Rep rows 2 and 3.

Row 14: Rep row 2, fasten off.

Rows 15–64: [Rep rows 5 to 14 consecutively] 5 times. At the end of row 64, **do not fasten off**, turn.

Row 65: Ch 1, sc in each dc and dc in each sc across, fasten off.

Border

Rnd 1: Attach light yellow with sl st in first sc of row 65, ch 1, (sc, ch 2, sc) in same sc as beg ch-1, *sk next 2 sts, **large shell** *(see Special Stitches)* in next st, sk next 2 sts**, sc in next st, rep from * across, ending last rep at **, (sc, ch 2, sc) in last sc; working in ends of rows, sc evenly sp across, (sc, ch 2, sc) in first ch of opposite side of foundation ch, rep from * across, ending last rep at **, (sc, ch 2, sc) in last st; working in ends of rows, sc in each st across, join in beg sc.

Rnd 2: Sl st in first ch-2 sp, ch 1, (sc, ch 2, sc, ch 3, sc, ch 2, sc) in corner ch-2 sp, *ch 4, (sc, ch 3, sc) in centre dc of next large shell, ch 4**, sc in next sc, rep from * across edge, ending last rep at **, (sc, ch 2, sc, ch 3, sc, ch 2, sc) in corner ch-2 sp, working across sc edge, ch 4, sk next 2 sc, [sl st in next sc, ch 4, sk next 2 sc] across to next corner ch-2 sp, (sc, ch 2, sc, ch 3, sc, ch 2, sc) in corner ch-2 sp, rep from * across, ending last rep at **, (sc, ch 2, sc, ch 3, sc, ch 2, sc) in corner ch-2 sp, ch 4, sk next 2 sc, [sl st in next sc, ch 4, sk next 2 sc] across edge, join in beg sc, fasten off. ■

Pastel Shells Afghan
Sample project was crocheted with Bernat Baby Coordinates, (75.2 per cent acrylic/22.2 per cent rayon/2.6 per cent nylon) from Spinrite.

BOOTIE BOUTIQUE

For a quick, last-minute baby shower gift, these simple yet sweet booties fit the bill perfectly. Make them in a rainbow of colours for a bootie bouquet!

Green V-Stitch

Design | Sue Childress

Skill Level
EASY

Finished Size
4 inches long

Materials
DK weight yarn:
　1 oz baby green
Size E/4/3.5mm crochet hook or size needed to obtain gauge
40 inches ¼-inch-wide green satin ribbon

Gauge
2 V-sts = 1¼ inches; 6 hdc = 1¼ inches
Check gauge to save time.

Notes
Weave in loose ends as work progresses.

Join rounds with a slip stitch unless otherwise stated.

Special Stitches
V-stitch (V-st): (Dc, ch 1, dc) in indicated st.

Beg V-stitch (beg V-st): Ch 4 *(counts as first dc and ch-1)*, dc in same st as beg ch-4.

Double treble decrease (dtr dec): *Yo hook 3 times, insert hook in ch-1 sp of next V-st, yo, draw up a lp, [yo, draw through 2 lps on hook] 3 times, rep from * 3 times *(5 lps on hook)*, yo, draw through all 5 lps on hook.

Bootie
Make 2

Rnd 1 (RS): Beg with sole, ch 16, 2 hdc in 3rd ch from hook, hdc in each of next 11 chs, 2 dc in next ch, 3 dc in last ch, working on opposite side of foundation ch, 2 dc in next ch, hdc in each of next 12 chs, **join** *(see Notes)* in top of beg ch. *(33 sts)*

Bootie Boutique
Sample projects were crocheted with
Red Heart Soft Baby (100 per cent
acrylic) from Coats & Clark.

Rnd 2: Ch 2 *(counts as first hdc throughout)*, hdc in same st as beg ch-2, 2 hdc in each of next 2 sts, hdc in each of next 10 sts, 2 dc in each of next 7 sts, hdc in each of next 12 sts, 2 hdc in next st, join in top of beg ch-2. *(44 sts)*

Rnd 3: Ch 3 *(counts as first dc)*, **bpdc** *(see Stitch Guide on page 126)* around each st around, join in 3rd ch of beg ch-3. *(44 bpdc)*

Rnd 4: Beg V-st *(see Special Stitches on page 84)* in first st, [sk next 2 sts, **V-st** *(see Special Stitches on page 84)* in next st] around, join in 3rd ch of beg ch-4. *(15 V-sts)*

Rnd 5: Sl st into ch-1 sp of V-st, beg V-st in same ch-1 sp, V-st in each of next 5 V-sts, **dtr dec** *(see Special Stitches on page 84)* in next 4 V-sts, V-st in each of next 5 V-sts, join in 3rd ch of beg V-st. *(11 V-sts, 1 dtr dec)*

Rnd 6: Sl st into ch-1 sp of V-st, beg V-st in same ch-1 sp, V-st in each of next 5 V-sts, V-st in top of dtr dec, V-st in each of next 5 V-sts, join in 3rd ch of beg V-st. *(12 V-sts)*

Rnd 7: Sl st into ch-1 sp of V-st, ch 1, sc in same ch-1 sp of V-st, 5 dc in ch-1 sp of next V-st, [sc in ch-1 sp of next V-st, 5 dc in ch-1 sp of next V-st] around, join in beg sc, fasten off.

Finishing

Cut green ribbon in half. Beg and ending at centre front, weave over and under dc sts of rnd 6, tie ends in a bow at centre front.

Blue Post-Stitch

Design | Sue Childress

Skill Level
EASY

Finished Size
3½ inches long

Materials
DK weight yarn:
    1 oz baby blue
Size E/4/3.5mm crochet hook or size needed to
    obtain gauge
40 inches ¼-inch-wide blue satin ribbon

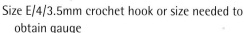

Gauge
6 dc = 1¼ inches
Check gauge to save time.

Notes
Weave in loose ends as work progresses.

Join rounds with a slip stitch unless otherwise stated.

Bootie
Make 2

Rnd 1: Ch 14, dc in 4th ch from hook, hdc in each of next 8 chs, 2 dc in next ch, 5 dc in last ch, working on opposite side of foundation ch, 2 dc in next ch, hdc in each of next 8 chs, 2 dc in same ch as beg st, **join** *(see Notes)* in top of beg dc. *(29 sts)*

Rnd 2: Ch 2 *(counts as first hdc)*, 3 hdc in next st, hdc in each of next 9 sts, 2 dc in each of next 7 sts, hdc in each of next 10 sts, 3 hdc in last st, join in top of beg ch-2. *(40 sts)*

Rnd 3: Ch 2, **bphdc** *(see Stitch Guide on page 126)* around each st around, join in top of beg ch-2.

Rnd 4: Ch 2, sk 2 top lps of bphdc and insert hook into horizontal bar at back of each st and hdc in each st around, join in top of beg ch-2.

Rnd 5: Ch 3 *(counts as first dc)*, 2 **fpdc** *(see Stitch Guide on page 126)* around same st as beg ch-3, sk next 2 sts, [3 fpdc around next st, sk next 3 sts] 9 times, sk next 2 sts, 3 fpdc around next st, join in top of beg ch-3. *(11 groups 3 fpdc)*

Rnd 6: Ch 1, sc in each of next 11 sts, [**dc dec** *(see Stitch Guide on page 126)* in next 3 sts] 3 times *(centre front toe dec)*, sc in each of next 13 sts, join in beg sc. *(27 sts)*

Rnd 7: Ch 1, sc in each of next 10 sts, [insert hook in next st, yo, draw up a lp] 3 times, yo, draw through all 4 lps on hook *(toe dec)*, sc in each of next 11 sts, join in beg sc. *(24 sc)*

Rnd 8: Ch 1, **reverse sc** *(Figure 1)* in each sc around, join in beg sc, fasten off.

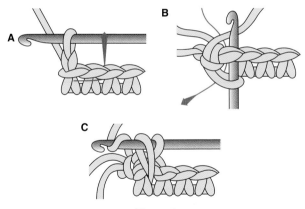

Figure 1
Reverse Single Crochet

Finishing

Cut baby blue ribbon in half. Beg and ending at centre front, weave ribbon over and under rnd 7 sc, tie ends in a bow at centre front.

Pink Love Knot

Design | Elizabeth Ann White

Skill Level
INTERMEDIATE

Finished Sizes
3½ and 4½-inch foot

Materials
DK weight yarn:
    ½ oz pink
Sizes B/1/2.25mm and C/2/2.75mm crochet hooks or sizes needed to obtain gauge
40 inches ¼-inch-wide white satin ribbon

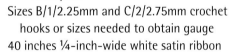

Gauge
Size B hook: 6 sts = 1 inch; 3 dc rows = 1 inch
Size C hook: 4 dc = 1 inch; 5 dc rows = 2 inches
Check gauge to save time.

Notes
Weave in loose ends as work progresses.

Join rounds with a slip stitch unless otherwise stated.

Use size B hook for 3½-inch foot and size C hook for 4½-inch foot.

Special Stitches

Love knot: *(Figure 2)* Draw up long lp in hook, yo, draw lp through, sc in back strand of long lp.

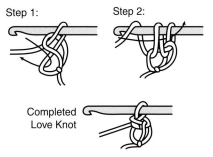

Figure 2
Love Knot

Double love knot: *(Figure 3)* [Draw up long lp on hook, yo, draw through, sc in back strand of long lp] twice.

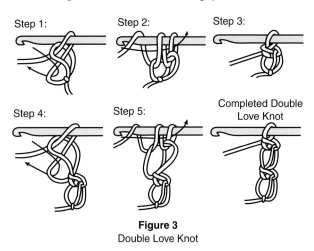

Figure 3
Double Love Knot

Bootie
Make 2

Rnd 1 (RS): Beg at toe end of foot, ch 4, 11 dc in 4th ch from hook, **join** *(see Notes)* in top of beg ch. *(12 dc)*

Rnd 2: Ch 3 *(counts as first dc throughout)*, dc in same st as beg ch-3, 2 dc in each rem st around, join in 3rd ch of beg ch-3. *(24 dc)*

Rnds 3–5: Ch 3, dc in each dc around, join in 3rd ch of beg ch-3.

Row 6: Now working in rows, ch 3, dc in each of next 23 dc, turn. *(24 dc)*

Rows 7–11: Ch 3, dc in each dc across, turn.

Row 12: Fold row 11 in half, working through both thicknesses, work 12 sl sts across, fasten off.

Cuff

Rnd 1: Attach yarn at centre back heel *(joining of row 12)*, ch 1, sc in same st as beg ch-1, work 35 sc evenly sp around ankle, join in beg sc. *(36 sc)*

Rnd 2: Ch 4 *(counts as first dc and ch-1)*, sk next sc, [dc in next sc, ch 1, sk next sc] around, join in 3rd ch of beg ch-4. *(18 dc, 18 ch-1 sps)*

Rnd 3: Sl st into next ch-1 sp ch 1, sc in same ch-1 sp, **double love knot** *(see Special Stitches)*, [sc in next ch-1 sp, double love knot] around, join in beg sc. *(18 sc, 18 double love knots)*

Rnd 4: Love knot *(see Special Stitches)*, sc in centre of first double love knot, double love knot, [sc in centre of next double love knot, double love knot] around, join, fasten off.

Finishing

Cut white ribbon in half. Beg and ending at centre front, weave ribbon over and under dc of rnd 2 of Cuff, tie ends in a bow at centre front. ■

HARVEST RUG

The warm colours of this rug will look inviting in the entrance to your home.

Design | Elaine Bartlett

Skill Level
EASY

Finished Size
27½ x 19½ inches

Materials
Worsted weight yarn (364 yds/198g per skein):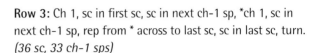
    2 skeins warm brown
    1 skein light yellow
Size N/13/9mm crochet hook or size needed to
    obtain gauge
Tapestry needle

Gauge
Working in pattern with 2 strands held tog: 6 sc and
    5 ch-1 sps = 4 inches; 12 pattern st rows = 4 inches

Notes
Weave in ends as work progresses.

Join rounds with a slip stitch unless otherwise stated.

Work with 2 strands of yarn held together throughout
unless otherwise stated.

Centre
Row 1 (RS): With warm brown, ch 70 loosely, sc in 2nd ch
from hook, sc in each rem ch across, turn. *(69 sc)*

Row 2: Ch 1, sc in first sc, *ch 1, sk next sc, sc in next sc,
rep from * across, turn. *(35 sc, 34 ch-1 sps)*

Row 3: Ch 1, sc in first sc, sc in next ch-1 sp, *ch 1, sc in
next ch-1 sp, rep from * across to last sc, sc in last sc, turn.
(36 sc, 33 ch-1 sps)

Row 4: Ch 1, sc in first sc, *ch 1, sc in next ch-1 sp, rep
from * across to last sc, ch 1, sc in last sc, turn. *(35 sc,
34 ch-1 sps)*

Row 5: Rep row 3. Fasten off.

Row 6: With light yellow, make slip knot on hook and
join with sc in first sc, *ch 1, sc in next ch-1 sp, rep from *
across to last sc, ch 1, sc in last sc, turn. *(35 sc, 34 ch-1 sps)*

Row 7: Rep row 3. Fasten off.

Row 8: With warm brown, rep row 6.

Rows 9–12: [Rep rows 3 and 4 alternately] twice.

Row 13: Rep row 3. Fasten off.

Rows 14–45: [Rep rows 6 to 13 consecutively] 4 times.
Fasten off.

Rows 46 & 47: Rep rows 6 and 7. Fasten off.

Row 48: With warm brown, rep row 6.

Rows 49 & 50: Rep rows 3 and 4.

Row 51: Rep row 3.

Row 52: Ch 1, sc in first sc, *sc in next ch-1 sp, sc in next
sc, rep from * across. Fasten off. *(69 sc)*

Edging

Rnd 1 (RS): Hold piece with RS facing, working across opposite side of foundation ch with light yellow, join with sc in first ch, *ch 1, sk next ch, sc in next ch, rep from * to last ch, (sc, ch 2, sc) in last ch *(corner)*, continuing along next side, **ch 1, sk next row, sc in end of next row, rep from ** across side, work (sc, ch 2, sc) *(corner)* in first sc of row 52, ***ch 1, sk next sc, sc in next sc, rep from *** to last sc, (sc, ch 2, sc) in last sc *(corner)*, continuing along next side, ****ch 1, sk next row, sc in end of next row, rep from **** across side to first sc, sc in same ch as first sc, ch 2, join in first sc. *(124 sc, 120 ch-1 sps, 4 ch-2 sps)*

Rnd 2: Sl st in next ch-1 sp, ch 1, sc in same ch-1 sp, *ch 1, sc in next ch-1 sp, rep from * around, working (sc, ch 2, sc) in each ch-2 corner sp, ch 1, join in first sc. Fasten off. *(128 sc, 124 ch-1 sps, 4 ch-2 sps)*

Rnd 3: With warm brown, join with sc in any ch-1 sp, *ch 1, sc in next ch-1 sp, rep from * around, working (sc, ch 2, sc) in each ch-2 corner sp, ch 1, join in first sc. Fasten off. *(132 sc, 128 ch-1 sps, 4 ch-2 sps)* ∎

Harvest Rug
Sample project was crocheted with Red Heart Super Saver (100 per cent acrylic) from Coats & Clark.

SEA BREEZE TABLE RUNNER

Set a summery table with the colours of the ocean flowing through this runner.

Design | Marty Miller

Skill Level

EASY

Finished Size

15 x 44 inches, excluding Fringe

Materials

Worsted weight yarn (178 yds/100g per skein):
  2 skeins each medium blue, cream and
    light blue
Size H/8/5mm crochet hook or size needed to
  obtain gauge
Tapestry needle

Gauge

19 sc = 4 inches; 21 rows = 4 inches

Notes

Two methods for beginning this table runner are given—the first method uses the traditional chain and first row of single crochet. The second method uses a foundation single crochet, which creates the chain and first row at the same time. Use either method.

Special Stitch

Foundation single crochet (foundation sc): Ch 2, insert hook in 2nd ch from hook, yo, draw up a lp, yo, draw through 1 lp on hook *(1 ch)*, yo, draw through 2 lps on hook *(foundation sc)*, insert hook under 2 lps of ch made in first foundation sc, yo, draw up a lp, yo, draw through 1 lp *(1 ch)*, yo, draw through 2 lps. *(2 foundation sc)*

Continue in this manner for number of foundation sc needed.

Method 1

Row 1 (WS): With medium blue, ch 201, sc in 2nd ch from hook, sc in each rem ch across. Fasten off, leaving an 8-inch end. *(200 sc)*

Method 2

Row 1 (WS): With medium blue, work 200 **foundation sc** *(see Special Stitch)*. Fasten off, leaving an 8-inch end. *(200 foundation sc)*

Both Methods

Row 2 (RS): With RS facing and leaving an 8-inch end, attach cream with sl st in first sc, ch 1, sc in same sc, ch 1, sk next sc, *sc in next sc, ch 1, rep from * across to last 2 sc, sc in each of last 2 sc. Fasten off, leaving an 8-inch end. Turn.

Row 3: Leaving an 8-inch end, attach light blue with sl st in first st, ch 1, sc in first sc, ch 1, *sk next sc, sc in next ch-1 sp, ch 1, rep from * across to last ch-1 sp, sc in last ch-1 sp, sc in last sc. Fasten off, leaving an 8-inch end. Turn.

Sea Breeze Table Runner
Sample project was crocheted with
TLC Cotton Plus (51 per cent cotton/
49 per cent acrylic) from Coats & Clark.

Rows 4–78: Rep row 3 in following colour sequence: 1 row medium blue, 1 row cream, 1 row light blue.

Row 79: Leaving an 8-inch end, attach medium blue with sl st in first sc, ch 1, sc in first sc, sc in each rem sc and in each ch-1 sp across, turn. *(200 sc)*

Row 80: Sl st in each st across. Fasten off, leaving an 8-inch end.

Edging

For piece started with Method 1, hold piece with RS facing and beg ch at top, attach medium blue with sl st in unused lp of first ch, sl st in each rem unused lp of beg ch. Fasten off, leaving an 8-inch end.

Fringe

Trim long yarn ends at ends of each row to 6 inches. ■

SIMPLY SWEET DOILIES

These delicate toppers will become keepsake treasures for generations to come.

Design | Katherine Eng

Skill Level
EASY

Finished Size
7½ inches in diameter

Materials
Size 10 crochet cotton (white: 400 yds per ball; solids: 350 yds per ball):
- 150 yds white
- 10 yds each rose and light blue

Size B/1/2.25mm crochet hook or size needed to obtain gauge

Tapestry needle

Gauge
Rnds 1–3 = 1¾ inches in diameter; [Dc, ch 2] 3 times = 1 inch

Notes
Weave in loose ends as work progresses.

Join rounds with a slip stitch unless otherwise stated.

Special Stitches
Small shell: 3 dc in st indicated.

Large shell: 5 dc in indicated st.

V-stitch (V-st): (Dc, ch 2, dc) in indicated st.

Doily
Rnd 1: Starting at centre, with white, ch 5, sl st to join in first ch to form a ring, ch 1, 12 sc in ring, join in beg sc. *(12 sc)*

Rnd 2: Ch 4 *(counts as first dc, ch-1)*, dc in same st as beg ch-4, ch 1, [(dc, ch 1, dc) in next sc, ch 1] around, join in 3rd ch of beg ch-4. *(24 dc)*

Rnd 3: Sl st in next ch-1 sp, ch 1, sc in same ch-1 sp as beg ch-1, *small shell *(see Special Stitches)* in next ch-1 sp**, sc in next ch-1 sp, rep from * around, ending last rep at **, join in beg sc. *(12 small shells, 12 sc)*

Rnd 4: Ch 5 *(counts as first dc, ch-2)*, sc in centre dc of small shell, ch 2, [dc in next sc, ch 2, sc in centre dc of small shell, ch 2] around, join in 3rd ch of beg ch-5. *(12 dc, 12 sc)*

Rnd 5: Ch 5, sk next ch-2 sp, dc in next sc, ch 2, [dc in next dc, ch 2, dc in next sc, ch 2] around, join in 3rd ch of beg ch-5. *(24 dc)*

Rnd 6: Ch 1, sc in same dc as beg ch-1, *large shell *(see Special Stitches)* in next dc**, sc in next dc, rep from * around, ending last rep at **, join in beg sc. *(12 large shells, 12 sc)*

Rnd 7: Ch 5, dc in same sc as beg ch-5, ch 2, *sc in centre dc of large shell, ch 2**, V-st *(see Special Stitches)* in next sc, ch 2, rep from * around, ending last rep at **, join in 3rd ch of beg ch-5. *(12 V-sts, 12 sc)*

Rnd 8: Ch 5, *dc in next dc, ch 2**, dc in next sc, ch 2, dc in next dc, ch 2, rep from * around, ending last rep at **, join in 3rd ch of beg ch-5. *(36 dc)*

Rnd 9: Rep rnd 6. *(18 large shells, 18 sc)*

Rnd 10: Rep rnd 7. *(18 V-sts, 18 sc)*

Rnd 11: Rep rnd 8. *(54 dc)*

Rnd 12: Ch 5, [dc in next dc, ch 2] around, join in 3rd ch of beg ch-5.

Rnd 13: Rep rnd 6, fasten off. *(27 large shells, 27 sc)*

Rnd 14: Attach rose *(light blue)* with sl st in any sc between large shells, ch 1, [sc in sc between large shells, sc in each of next 2 dc, 3 sc in next dc, sc in each of next 2 dc] around, join in beg sc, fasten off. *(224 sc)*

Rnd 15: Attach white with sl st in same sc as beg of previous rnd, ch 1, sc in same sc as beg ch-1, *ch 1, sk next 2 sc, (sc, ch 2, sc) in next sc, (sc, ch 3, sc) in next sc, (sc, ch 2, sc) in next sc, ch 1, sk next 2 sc**, sc in next sc, rep from * around, ending last rep at **, join in beg sc, fasten off. *(189 sc, 27 ch-3 sps, 54 ch-2 sps)* ■

Simply Sweet Doilies

Sample project was crocheted with Aunt Lydia's Classic size 10 crochet cotton (100 per cent mercerized cotton) from Coats & Clark.

SOFT PASTELS BASKETS

Use these glorious pastel baskets as plant-pot covers, candy holders, loose change receptacles—anything your heart desires!

Design | Katherine Eng

Skill Level

EASY

Finished Size

5 x 7 inches

Materials

Worsted weight yarn (solid: 364 yds/198g per skein; multi: 224 yds/141g per skein):

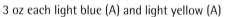

MEDIUM

   3 oz each light blue (A) and light yellow (A)

   1½ oz each variegated blue shades (B) and variegated yellow shades (B)

Size H/8/5mm crochet hook or size needed to obtain gauge

Tapestry needle

Gauge

Rnds 1 and 2 = 2¼ inches

Notes

Weave in loose ends as work progresses.

Join rounds with a slip stitch unless otherwise stated.

Materials listed will make 2 baskets. For blue basket, use light blue and variegated blue shades. For yellow basket, use light yellow and variegated yellow shades.

Special Stitches

Shell: 5 dc in indicated st.

Popcorn (pc): 4 dc in indicated st, draw up a lp, remove hook, insert hook in first dc of 4-dc group, pick up dropped lp and draw through st on hook.

Basket

Rnd 1: With 2 strands A and 1 strand B, ch 4, **join** *(see Notes)* in first ch to form a ring, ch 1, 8 sc in ring, join in beg sc. *(8 sc)*

Rnd 2: Ch 1, 2 sc in each sc around, join in beg sc. *(16 sc)*

Rnd 3: Ch 1, [sc in next sc, 2 sc in next sc] around, join in beg sc. *(24 sc)*

Rnd 4: Ch 1, [sc in each of next 3 sc, 2 sc in next sc] around, join in beg sc. *(30 sc)*

Rnd 5: Rep rnd 3. *(45 sc)*

Rnds 6–8: Ch 1, sc in each sc around, join in beg sc.

Rnd 9: Ch 1, sc in same sc as beg ch-1, *sk next 2 sc, **shell** *(see Special Stitches)* in next sc, sk next sc**, sc in next sc, rep from * around, ending last rep at **, join in beg sc. *(9 shells, 9 sc)*

Rnd 10: Ch 3 *(counts as first dc)*, 3 dc in same st as beg ch-3, draw up a lp, remove hook, insert hook in 3rd ch of beg ch-3, pick up dropped lp, draw through st on hook *(beg pc)*, *ch 2, sc in centre dc of next shell, ch 2**, **pc** *(see Special Stitches)* in next sc, rep from * around, ending last rep at **, join in 3rd ch of beg ch-3. *(9 pc, 9 sc)*

Rnd 11: Ch 1, sc in **back lp** *(see Stitch Guide on page 126)* of pc, shell in next sc, *sc in back lp of next pc, shell in next sc, rep from * around, join in beg sc. *(9 shells, 9 sc)*

Rnds 12 & 13: Rep rnds 10 and 11.

Rnd 14: *Ch 2, sk 1 dc, sl st in next dc, ch 3, sc in first ch of ch-3, sk next dc, sl st in next dc, ch 2, sk next dc, sl st in next sc, rep from * around, fasten off. ∎

Soft Pastels Baskets
Sample project was crocheted with Red Heart Super Saver (100 per cent acrylic) from Coats & Clark.

CLASSY CABLES PILLOW

Add a distinctive touch to any room with this pillow that features a unique cable design.

Design | Darla Sims

Skill Level

INTERMEDIATE

Finished Size

18 x 18 inches

Materials

Worsted weight yarn (312 yds/170g per skein):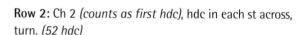
    4 skeins light celery
Sizes G/6/4mm and H/8/5mm crochet hooks or
    sizes needed to obtain gauge
Yarn needle
Stitch markers
18 x 18-inch pillow form

Gauge

Size G hook: 4 sc = 1 inch
Size H hook: 7 hdc = 2 inches

Notes

Weave in loose ends as work progresses.

Join rounds with a slip stitch unless otherwise stated.

Pillow cover is smaller than actual pillow form and is necessary for cover to fit snuggly and stay in place.

Front

Row 1: Starting at bottom edge with size H hook, ch 53, hdc in 3rd ch from hook *(2 sk chs count as first hdc)*, hdc in each rem ch across, turn. *(52 hdc)*

Row 2: Ch 2 *(counts as first hdc)*, hdc in each st across, turn. *(52 hdc)*

Row 3: Ch 2, hdc in next st, *sk next st, [**fpdc** *(see Stitch Guide on page 126)* in next hdc of row 1, sk st directly behind post st] twice, fpdc in hdc directly below sk hdc, hdc in each of next 2 hdc, rep from * across, turn. *(10 cables, 22 hdc)*

Row 4: Rep row 2.

Row 5: Ch 2, hdc in next hdc, [fpdc in each of next 3 fpdc, hdc in each of next 2 hdc] 10 times, turn.

Row 6: Rep row 2.

Row 7: Ch 2, hdc in next hdc, *sk next fpdc, fpdc in each of next 2 fpdc, fpdc in sk fpdc, hdc in each of next 2 hdc, rep from * across, turn. *(10 cables, 22 hdc)*

Rows 8–47: [Rep rows 4 to 7 consecutively] 10 times. At the end of row 47, fasten off.

Back

Rows 1–47: Rep rows 1 to 47 of Front. At the end of row 47, turn, do not fasten off.

Flap

Row 1: With size H hook, ch 1, **hdc dec** *(see Stitch Guide on page 126)* in next 2 sts, hdc in each st across to last 2 sts, hdc dec in last 2 sts, turn. *(50 hdc)*

Row 2: Ch 1, hdc dec in next 2 sts, hdc in each st across to last 2 sts, hdc dec in last 2 sts, turn. *(48 hdc)*

Rows 3–25: Rep row 2. *(2 hdc)*

Row 26: Ch 1, hdc dec in next 2 sts, fasten off. *(1 hdc)*

Flap Edging

Row 1 (RS): With size G hook, attach yarn with sc in side edge of row 1 of Flap, work 42 sc across side edge to row 26, 3 sc in hdc of row 26, work 43 sc across opposite edge of Flap.

Row 2: Ch 1, **reverse sc** *(Figure 1)* in each sc of row 1 of Flap Edging, fasten off.

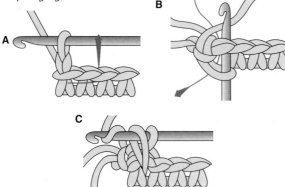

Figure 1
Reverse Single Crochet

Frog

Loop Piece

With size G hook, make a ch approximately 18 inches in length, sl st in 2nd ch from hook, sl st in each ch across, leaving a 12-inch length of yarn, fasten off. Using photo as a guide, form lp first, then frog, securing as you go with

yarn threaded into yarn needle inserting needle between sts as you tack into place, form rem 2 lps.

Button Piece

With size G hook, make a ch approximately 18 inches in length, sl st in 2nd ch from hook, sl st in each ch across, leaving a 12-inch length of yarn, fasten off. Using photo as a guide, beg with double knot at end for button closure, shape and sew rem 3 lps as for Loop Piece.

Finishing

With long length of yarn, sew Front and Back tog on sides and bottom edge, leaving Flap free, insert pillow form. Working through top lps of Front and ridge on WS of last cable row of Back, sew opening closed. Sew Frog to front of Flap. ∎

COUNTRY LACE AFGHAN

Crocheters of all skill levels will love this V-stitch and cluster afghan, crocheted in a yummy dark orchid-coloured yarn.

Design | Agnes Russell

Skill Level
BEGINNER

Finished Size
44 x 62 inches, excluding Fringe

Materials
Worsted weight yarn (364 yds/198g per skein):
    5 skeins dark orchid
Size H/8/5mm crochet hook or size needed to
   obtain gauge
Tapestry needle

Gauge
[1 V-st, 3-tr cl] twice = 5½ inches; 3 rows = 3½ inches

Notes
Weave in loose ends as work progresses.

To avoid knots within the afghan, always start a new skein at the beginning of a row.

Chain-4 counts as first treble throughout.

Special Stitches
V-stitch (V-st): (Tr, ch 1, tr) in indicated st.

3-treble crochet cluster (3-tr cl): *Yo hook twice, insert hook in indicated st, yo, draw up lp, [yo, draw through 2 lps on hook] twice, rep from * twice in same st, yo, draw through all 4 lps on hook.

Afghan
Row 1: Ch 100, **3-tr cl** *(see Special Stitches)* in 7th ch from hook, (ch 3, 3-tr cl) twice in same ch as previous 3-tr cl, sk next 2 chs, [**V-st** *(see Special Stitches)* in next ch, sk next 2 chs, 3-tr cl in next ch, (ch 3, 3-tr cl) twice in same ch as previous 3-tr cl, sk next 2 chs] 15 times, tr in last ch, turn. *(16 groups of 3-tr cls, 15 V-sts, 2 tr)*

Row 2: Ch 4, *sk first 3-tr cl, sk next ch-3 sp, tr in next 3-tr cl, (ch 3, tr) twice in same 3-tr cl as previous tr**, V-st in next ch-1 sp of V-st, rep from * across, ending last rep at **, tr in end tr, turn.

Row 3: Ch 4, * sk next tr, sk next ch-3 sp, 3-tr cl in centre tr, (ch 3, 3-tr cl) twice in same centre tr as previous 3-tr cl**, V-st in next ch-1 sp of V-st, rep from * across, ending last rep at **, tr in end tr, turn.

Rows 4–59: [Rep rows 2 and 3 alternately] 28 times.

Row 60: Rep Row 2.

Row 61: Ch 1, sc in end tr, *ch 3, sk next tr, sk next ch-3 sp, sc in next centre tr, ch 3**, sc in ch-1 sp of next V-st, rep from * across, ending last rep at **, sc in end tr, fasten off.

Fringe

Cut 7 strands each 16 inches long for each Fringe group. Cut 31 groups of 7 strands for both top and bottom of Afghan.

Bottom Fringe groups are worked in opposite side of foundation ch in base of 3-tr cl and V-sts. Working across top around sc row (Row 61), attach a Fringe group in ch sp of each V-st and centre tr of each 3-tr group.

[Fold each 7-strand group in half, insert hook, draw strands through at fold to form a lp on hook, draw cut ends through lp on hook, pull strands to tighten] rep in each indicated st. Trim ends. ■

Country Lace Afghan
Sample project was crocheted with Red Heart Super Saver (100 per cent acrylic) from Coats & Clark.

CROSSHATCH STITCH AFGHAN

This beautiful blue afghan is made out of lightweight yarn, making it perfect for a cool summer evening.

Design | Nancy Nehring

Skill Level

EASY

Finished Size

34 x 42 inches

Materials

Sport weight yarn (235 yds/50g per ball):
   4 balls light blue
Size K/10½/6.5 mm crochet hook or size needed
   to obtain gauge
Tapestry needle

2
FINE

Gauge

1 crosshatch st = 2 inches

Note: *Crosshatch st is extremely flexible making it difficult to measure gauge. Matching gauge is not critical; if gauge is tighter, additional yarn may be needed.*

Notes

Weave in ends as work progresses.

Chain-3 at beginning of double crochet row counts as first double crochet unless otherwise stated.

Special Stitch

Crosshatch stitch (crosshatch st): (Sc, ch 2, 3 dc) in indicated sp.

Afghan

Row 1 (RS): Ch 152, 2 dc in 4th ch from hook *(beg 3 sk chs count as a dc)*, *sk next 3 chs, sc in next ch, ch 2, dc in each of next 3 chs, rep from * 20 times, sc in last ch, turn. *(66 dc, 21 sc, 21 ch-1 sps)*

Row 2: Ch 3 *(see Notes)*, 2 dc in first sc, sk next 3 dc, **crosshatch st** *(see Special Stitch)* in next ch-2 sp, *sk next sc and next 3 dc, crosshatch st in next ch-2 sp, rep from * 19 times, sc in sp formed by beg 3 sk chs, turn. *(21 crosshatch sts, 3 dc, 1 sc)*

Row 3: 2 dc in first sc, sk next 3 dc, crosshatch st in ch-2 sp of next crosshatch st, *sk next sc and next 3 dc, crosshatch st in ch-2 sp of next crosshatch st, rep from * 19 times, sc in sp formed by beg ch-3, turn.

Rows 4–62: Rep row 3. At end of last row, fasten off. ■

Crosshatch Stitch Afghan
Sample project was crocheted
with Patons Lacette, (39 per cent
nylon/36 per cent acrylic/25 per
cent mohair) from Spinrite.

ONE ROW THROW

The bulky weight yarn used in this throw makes it ideal for those long winter nights spent snuggling up by the fireplace.

Design | Cindy Adams

Skill Level

EASY

Finished Size
48 x 60 inches

Materials
Chunky weight yarn (148 yds/100g per ball):
    11 balls rust/blue variegated
    1 ball rust
Size J/10/6mm crochet hook or size needed to
    obtain gauge
Tapestry needle

Gauge
(Sc, ch 3, 3 dc) = 2 inches

Note
Weave in ends as work progresses.

Centre
Row 1: With rust/blue variegated, ch 166, sc in 2nd ch from hook, sk next 2 chs, 3 dc in next ch, *ch 3, sk next 3 chs, sc in next ch, sk next 2 chs, 3 dc in next ch, rep from * across, turn. *(24 sc, 72 dc, 24 ch-3 sps)*

Row 2: Ch 1, sc in first dc, 3 dc in next sc, *ch 3, sc in next ch-3 sp, 3 dc in next sc, rep from * across, turn.

Rep row 2 until piece measures 59 inches.

Last row: Ch 1, sc in first dc, 3 dc in next sc, *ch 3, sc in next ch-3 sp, 3 dc in next sc, rep from * across, **change colour** *(see Stitch Guide on page 126)* to rust in last sc, turn.

Edging
Ch 1, sc in first dc, 3 dc in next sc, *ch 3, sc in next ch-3 sp, 3 dc in next sc, rep from * across, working across next side in ends of rows, **sc in end of next sc row, 3 dc in end of next dc row, ch 3, rep from ** to last sc row, sc in end of last sc row, sk next dc, row, 3 dc in last sc row, ch 3, working across next side, sc in sp formed by next 3 sk chs of row 1, ***dc in unused lp of ch at base of next 3-dc group on row 1, ch 3, sc in sp formed by next 3 sk chs of row 1, rep from *** to last 3 sk chs of row 1, 3 dc in sp formed by last 3 sk chs, ch 3, working across next side in ends of rows, ****sc in end of row 1, 3 dc in end of next dc row, ch 3, rep from **** to last sc row, sc in end of last sc row, 3 dc in side of first sc, fasten off. ∎

One Row Throw
Sample project was crocheted with
Patons Shetland Chunky (75 per cent
acrylic/25 per cent wool) from Spinrite.

SHADES OF AUTUMN

This colourful afghan is sure to bring back memories of walking through crunchy leaves on a crisp fall day.

Design | Rhonda Dodds

Skill Level

◼☐☐☐
BEGINNER

Finished Size
42 x 52 inches

Materials

Chunky weight yarn (153 yds/140g per ball):
   8 balls brown
Chunky weight yarn (135 yds/85g per ball):
   4 balls avocado
   2 balls paprika
Size P/15/10mm crochet hook or size needed to obtain gauge
Tapestry needle

Gauge
With 2 strands of yarn held tog: Square = 9½ inches

Notes
Weave in ends as work progresses.

Entire afghan is worked with 2 strands of yarn held together.

Join rounds with a slip stitch unless otherwise stated.

Chain-3 at beginning of double crochet round counts as first double crochet unless otherwise stated.

Special Stitch
Cross-stitch (cross-st): Sk indicated st, dc in next st, working in dc just made, dc in sk st.

Square
Make 20

Rnd 1 (RS): With paprika, ch 5, join in first ch to form a ring, **ch 3** *(see Notes)*, 3 dc in ring, ch 2, [4 dc in ring, ch 2] 3 times, join in 3rd ch of beg ch-3, fasten off. *(16 dc, 4 ch-2 sps)*

Rnd 2: Join avocado in any ch-2 sp, ch 3, (dc, ch 2, 2 dc) in same sp *(beg corner)*, [dc in each of next 4 dc, (2 dc, ch 2, 2 dc) in next ch-2 sp *(corner)*] twice, dc in each of next 4 sc, join in 3rd ch of beg ch-3, fasten off. *(32 dc, 4 ch-2 sps)*

Rnd 3: Join brown in any corner ch-2 sp, ch 1, 3 sc in same sp *(sc corner)*, [sc in each of next 8 dc, 3 sc in next corner ch-2 sp (sc corner)] twice, sc in each of next 8 dc, join in first sc. *(50 sc)*

Rnd 4: Sl st in next sc, ch 3, (dc, ch 2, 2 dc) in same sc *(beg corner)*, *[**cross-st** *(see Special Stitch)* in next 2 sc] 5 times, (2 dc, ch 2, 2 dc) in next sc *(corner)*, rep from * twice, [cross-st in next 2 sc] 5 times, join in 3rd ch of beg ch 3, fasten off. *(20 cross-sts, 4 ch-2 sps)*

Shades of Autumn

Sample project was crocheted with Wool-Ease Chunky (80 per cent acrylic/ 20 per cent wool) and Jiffy (100 per cent acrylic) from Lion Brand.

Assembly

With tapestry needle and brown and working in **back lps** *(see Stitch Guide on page 126)* only, sew Squares tog with RS facing, carefully matching sts. Sew Squares tog in 5 rows of 4 Squares each.

Border

Rnd 1 (RS): With RS facing, join paprika in any corner ch-2 sp, ch 1, 3 sc in same sp *(corner)*, *sc evenly sp to next corner ch-2 sp, 3 sc in corner sp *(corner)*, rep from * twice, sc evenly sp to first sc, join in first sc, fasten off.

Rnd 2: Join avocado in 2nd sc of any corner, ch 1, 3 sc in same sc *(corner)*, *sc in each sc to 2nd sc of next corner, 3 sc in 2nd sc *(corner)*, rep from * twice, sc in each sc to first sc, join in first sc, fasten off.

Rnd 3: Join brown in any sc, ch 3, cross-st in next 2 sc, *sk next sc, dc in next sc, cross-st in next 2 sc, rep from * around to beg ch-3, join in 3rd ch of beg ch-3, fasten off. ■

GRANNY SQUARE DISHCLOTH

Stitch up one of these cute dishcloths for a quick hostess gift to give at your next party.

Design | Katherine Eng

Skill Level

EASY

Finished Size
10 inches square

Materials
Worsted weight yarn (122 yds/70g per ball):

4

MEDIUM

1 ball each white, light blue and delft blue
Size F/5/3.75mm crochet hook or size needed to obtain gauge
Tapestry needle

Gauge
Block = 2¾ inches square

Notes
Join with slip stitch as indicated unless otherwise stated.

Chain-3 at beginning of round counts as first double crochet unless otherwise stated.

Block
Make 9

Rnd 1: With delft blue, ch 4, **join** *(see Notes)* in beg ch to form ring, **ch 3** *(see Notes)*, 2 dc in ring, ch 2, (3 dc in ring, ch 2) 3 times, join in 3rd ch of beg ch-3. Fasten off. *(12 dc, 4 ch sps)*

Rnd 2: Join white in any corner ch sp, (ch 3, 2 dc, ch 2, 3 dc) in same sp, ch 1, *(3 dc, ch 2, 3 dc) in next ch sp, ch 1, rep from * around, join in 3rd ch of beg ch-3. Fasten off.

Rnd 3: Join light blue with sc in any corner ch sp, (sc, ch 3, 2 sc) in same sp, *ch 1, sk next st, sc in next st, ch 1, sk next st, 2 sc in next ch-1 sp, ch 1, sk next st, sc in next st, ch 1, sk next st**, (2 sc, ch 3, 2 sc) in next corner ch sp, rep from * around ending last rep at **, join in beg sc. Fasten off.

Separate a strand of light blue into 2-ply lengths.

Hold Blocks WS tog, matching sts, with 2-ply strand, sew tog through **back lps** *(see Stitch Guide on page 126)* in 3 rows of 3 blocks each.

Border
Rnd 1: Join light blue with sc in any corner ch sp, (ch 3, sc) in same sp, *[ch 2, sc in next ch sp, ch 1, sc in next ch sp, ch 2, sc in next ch sp, ch 1, sc in next ch sp, ch 2, sc in next ch sp before next seam, ch 1, sc in next ch sp after same seam] twice, [ch 2, sc in next ch sp, ch 1, sc in next ch sp] twice, ch 2**, (sc, ch 3, sc) in next corner ch sp, rep from * around ending last rep at **, join in beg sc. Fasten off.

Rnd 2: Join white with sc in any corner ch sp, (ch 3, sc) in same sp, *sc in next st, [ch 2, sc in next st, ch 1, sc in next st] 8 times, ch 2, sc in next st**, (sc, ch 3, sc) in next corner ch sp, rep from * around, ending last rep at **, join in beg sc. Fasten off.

Rnd 3: Join delft blue in any corner ch sp, (ch 3, sl st, ch 4, sl st, ch 3, sl st) in same sp, *ch 2, (sl st, ch 3, sl st) in next ch-2 sp, [ch 2, sl st in next ch-1 sp, ch 2, (sl st, ch 3, sl st) in next ch-2 sp] across to next corner ch sp**, (sl st, ch 3, sl st, ch 4, sl st, ch 3, sl st) in next corner ch sp, rep from * around, ending last rep at **, join in beg sl st. Fasten off. ∎

Granny Square Dishcloth

Sample project was crocheted with Peaches & Crème cotton yarn (100 per cent cotton) from Pisgah Yarn & Dyeing Co. Inc.

PLASTIC BAG HOLDER

This handy holder is a must for any kitchen. It is both practical and charming.

Design | Tara Surprenant

Skill Level
EASY

Finished Size
16 inches long

Materials
Worsted weight yarn:
    6 oz/300 yds/170g black
    5 yds each oatmeal, orange, lime green
Size I/9/5.5mm crochet hook or size needed to
    obtain gauge
Tapestry needle
1½-inch diameter ponytail holders: 2

Gauge
10 dc = 1 inch; 2 dc rows = 1 inch

Notes
Weave in ends as work progresses.

Join rounds with a slip stitch unless otherwise stated.

Bag Holder
Rnd 1 (RS): With black, ch 35, join in first ch to form a ring, ch 1, sc in each ch, join in first sc. *(35 sc)*

Rnd 2: Ch 1, working over 1 ponytail holder, sc in each sc around, join in first sc.

Rnd 3: Ch 2, dc in first sc and in each rem sc around, join in first dc.

Rnd 4: Ch 2, dc in first dc and in each rem dc around, join in first dc.

Rnds 5–30: Rep rnd 4.

Rnd 31: Ch 1, working over 2nd ponytail holder, sc in each dc around, join in first sc.

Rnd 32: Ch 1, sc in first dc, ch 10 *(hanging lp)*, sc in each rem sc around, join in first sc, fasten off.

Flower
Make 2

Rnd 1 (RS): With orange, ch 3, join in first ch to form a ring, ch 4 *(counts as first dc and ch-2 sp)*, [dc in ring, ch 2] 5 times, join in 2nd ch of beg ch-4. *(6 dc, 6 ch-2 sps)*

Rnd 2: Ch 1, in each ch-2 sp work (sc, 3 dc, sc) *(petal)*, join in first sc. *(6 petals)*

Rnd 3: Holding petals made on rnd 2 to front, sl st in back of beg ch-4 of rnd 1, *ch 5, sl st in next dc on rnd 1, rep from * around, join in first sl st, fasten off. *(6 sl sts, 6 ch-5 sps)*

Rnd 4: Join oatmeal in first ch-5 sp, in next ch-5 sp work (dc, 5 tr, dc) *(large petal)*, *sl st in next ch-5 sp, in next ch-5 sp work (dc, 5 tr, dc) *(large petal)*, rep from * 4 times, join in joining sl st, fasten off, leaving an 8-inch end for sewing.

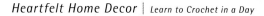

Leaf
Make 4

With lime green, ch 10, working in **back lps** *(see Stitch Guide on page 126)* only, sc in 2nd ch from hook, sc in next ch, ch 1, dc in each of next 2 chs, tr in each of next 3 chs, dc in next ch, 2 dc in last ch, working in unused lps on opposite side of foundation ch, 2 dc in first ch, dc in next ch, tr in each of next 3 chs, dc in each of next 2 chs, sc in each of last 2 chs, join in first sc, fasten off, leaving an 8-inch end for sewing.

Finishing

Referring to photo for placement, sew Flowers and Leaves to Bag Holder. ■

Plastic Bag Holder

Sample project was crocheted with Red Heart Super Saver (100 per cent acrylic) from Coats & Clark.

TOWEL EDGINGS

Get ready for company by dressing up your kitchen towels with one of these quick-to-stitch edgings.

Design | Jo Ann Loftis

Blue Towel Edging

Skill Level

EASY

Finished Size
1 inch wide

Materials
Worsted weight yarn (122 yds/71g per ball):
    1 ball light blue
Size I/9/5.5mm crochet hook or size needed to
    obtain gauge
Tapestry needle
Sewing needle
Cotton dish towel
Matching sewing thread

4
MEDIUM

Gauge
4 sts = 1 inch

Note
Weave in ends as work progresses.

Instructions

Row 1 (WS): Make ch to desired length in multiple of 6 plus 2 at end, sc in 2nd ch from hook, sc in each rem ch across, turn.

Row 2 (RS): Ch 1, sc in first sc, *sk next 2 sc, 5 dc in next sc, sk next 2 sc, sc in next sc, rep from * across, fasten off.

Finishing
Sew Edging to 1 short end of towel.

Towel Edgings
Sample project was crocheted with Peaches & Crème (100 per cent cotton) from Elmore-Pisgah.

Chocolate Towel Edging

Skill Level EASY

Finished Size
1½ inch wide

Materials
Worsted weight yarn (122 yds/71g per ball):
   1 ball chocolate
Size I/9/5.5mm crochet hook or size needed to
   obtain gauge
Tapestry needle
Sewing needle
Cotton dish towel
Matching sewing thread

4 MEDIUM

Gauge
4 sts = 1 inch

Note
Weave in ends as work progresses.

Instructions
Row 1 (WS): Make ch to desired length in multiple of 8 plus 2 at end, sc in 2nd ch from hook, sc in each rem ch across, turn.

Row 2 (RS): Ch 1, sc in first sc, *sk next 3 sc, (tr, ch 1) 6 times in next sc, tr in same sc, sk next 3 sc, sc in next sc, rep from * across, fasten off.

Finishing
Sew piece to 1 short end of towel.

Yellow & White Towel Edging

Skill Level EASY

Finished Size
1⅝ inch wide

Materials
Worsted weight yarn (122 yds/71g per ball):
   1 ball each yellow and white
Size I/9/5.5mm crochet hook or size needed to
   obtain gauge
Tapestry needle
Sewing needle
Cotton dish towel
Matching sewing thread

4 MEDIUM

Gauge
4 sts = 1 inch

Note
Weave in ends as work progresses.

Instructions
Row 1 (RS): With yellow, make ch to desired length in multiple of 7 plus 1 at end, sc in 2nd ch from hook, sc in each rem ch across, turn.

Row 2: Ch 1, sc in first sc, 2 dc in next sc, 2 tr in next sc, 2 dtr in next sc, 2 tr in next sc, 2 dc in next sc, sc in next sc, *sc in next sc, 2 dc in next sc, 2 tr in next sc, 2 dtr in next sc, 2 tr in next sc, 2 dc in next sc, sc in next sc, rep from * across, fasten off.

Row 3: With white, make slip knot on hook and join with sc in first sc, sc in each rem sc across, fasten off.

Finishing
Sew piece to 1 short end of towel.

White & Daisy Ombré Towel Edging

Skill Level
EASY

Finished Size
1½ inch wide

Materials
Worsted weight yarn (solid: 122 yds/ 71g per ball; ombre: 98 yds/57g per ball):
    1 ball each white and daisy ombre
Size I/9/5.5mm crochet hook or size needed to obtain gauge
Tapestry needle
Sewing needle
Cotton dish towel
Matching sewing thread

Gauge
4 sts = 1 inch

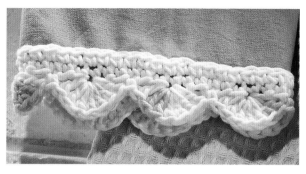

Notes
Weave in ends as work progresses.

Join rounds with a slip stitch unless otherwise stated.

Instructions
Rnd 1 (RS): With white, make ch to desired length in multiple of 6 plus 1 at end, 3 sc in 2nd ch from hook, sc in each ch to last ch, 3 sc in last ch, working in unused lps on opposite side of foundation ch, sc in each ch across, join in beg ch-1, fasten off.

Row 2: Now working in rows, with daisy ombré, make slip knot on hook and join with sc in 2nd sc, *sk next 2 sc, 7 dc in next sc, sk next 2 sc, sc in next sc, rep from * to first sc of last 3-sc group, fasten off, leaving rem sc unworked.

Finishing
Sew piece to 1 short end of towel. ■

INDEX

INDEX

Heartfelt Home Decor

Harvest Rug, 89

Classy Cables Pillow, 100

Sea Breeze Table Runner, 92

Simply Sweet Doilies, 95

Soft Pastels Baskets, 98

Country Lace Afghan, 103

Crosshatch Stitch
Afghan, 106

One Row Throw, 108

Plastic Bag Holder, 116

Towel Edgings, 118

Shades of Autumn, 110

Granny Square
Dishcloth, 113

GENERAL INFORMATION

Standard Yarn Weight System
Categories of yarn, gauge ranges, and recommended needle sizes

Yarn Weight Symbol & Category Names	1 SUPER FINE	2 FINE	3 LIGHT	4 MEDIUM	5 BULKY	6 SUPER BULKY
Type of Yarns in Category	Sock, Fingering, Baby	Sport, Baby	DK, Light Worsted	Worsted, Afghan, Aran	Chunky, Craft, Rug	Bulky, Roving
Knit Gauge* Ranges in Stockinette Stitch to 4 inches	21–32 sts	23–26 sts	21–24 sts	16–20 sts	12–15 sts	6–11 sts
Recommended Needle in Metric Size Range	2.25–3.25mm	3.25–3.75mm	3.75–4.5mm	4.5–5.5mm	5.5–8mm	8mm
Recommended Needle Canada/U.S. Size Range	1 to 3	3 to 5	5 to 7	7 to 9	9 to 11	11 and larger

* GUIDELINES ONLY: The above reflect the most commonly used gauges and needle sizes for specific yarn categories.

Skill Levels

BEGINNER

Projects for first-time knitters using basic knit and purl stitches. Minimal shaping.

EASY

Projects using basic stitches, repetitive stitch patterns, simple colour changes and simple shaping and finishing.

INTERMEDIATE

Projects with a variety of stitches, such as basic cables and lace, simple intarsia, double-pointed needles and knitting in the round needle techniques, mid-level shaping and finishing.

EXPERIENCED

Projects using advanced techniques and stitches, such as short rows, Fair Isle, more intricate intarsia, cables, lace patterns and numerous colour changes.

Metric Conversion Charts

METRIC CONVERSIONS

yards	x	.9144	=	metres (m)
yards	x	91.44	=	centimetres (cm)
inches	x	2.54	=	centimetres (cm)
inches	x	25.40	=	millimetres (mm)
inches	x	.0254	=	metres (m)

centimetres	x	.3937	=	inches
metres	x	1.0936	=	yards

INCHES INTO MILLIMETRES & CENTIMETRES (Rounded off slightly)

inches	mm	cm	inches	cm	inches	cm	inches	cm
1/8	3	0.3	5	12.5	21	53.5	38	96.5
1/4	6	0.6	5 1/2	14	22	56	39	99
3/8	10	1	6	15	23	58.5	40	101.5
1/2	13	1.3	7	18	24	61	41	104
5/8	15	1.5	8	20.5	25	63.5	42	106.5
3/4	20	2	9	23	26	66	43	109
7/8	22	2.2	10	25.5	27	68.5	44	112
1	25	2.5	11	28	28	71	45	114.5
1 1/4	32	3.2	12	30.5	29	73.5	46	117
1 1/2	38	3.8	13	33	30	76	47	119.5
1 3/4	45	4.5	14	35.5	31	79	48	122
2	50	5	15	38	32	81.5	49	124.5
2 1/2	65	6.5	16	40.5	33	84	50	127
3	75	7.5	17	43	34	86.5		
3 1/2	90	9	18	46	35	89		
4	100	10	19	48.5	36	91.5		
4 1/2	115	11.5	20	51	37	94		

KNITTING NEEDLES CONVERSION CHART

Canada/U.S.	0	1	2	3	4	5	6	7	8	9	10	10½	11	13	15
Metric (mm)	2	2¼	2¾	3¼	3½	3¾	4	4½	5	5½	6	6½	8	9	10

CROCHET HOOKS CONVERSION CHART

Canada/U.S.	1/B	2/C	3/D	4/E	5/F	6/G	8/H	9/I	10/J	10½/K	N
Metric (mm)	2.25	2.75	3.25	3.5	3.75	4.25	5	5.5	6	6.5	9.0

STITCH GUIDE

Chain (ch): Yo, pull through lp on hook.

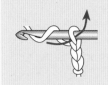

Slip stitch (sl st): Insert hook in st, pull through both lps on hook.

Front loop (front lp) Back loop (back lp)

Front Loop   Back Loop

Single crochet (sc): Insert hook in st, yo, pull through st, yo, pull through both lps on hook.

Front post stitch (fp): Back post stitch (bp): When working post st, insert hook from right to left around post st on previous row.

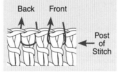

Back   Front

Post of Stitch

Half double crochet (hdc): Yo, insert hook in st, yo, pull through st, yo, pull through all 3 lps on hook.

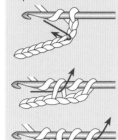

Double treble crochet (dtr): Yo 3 times, insert hook in st, yo, pull through st, [yo, pull through 2 lps] 4 times.

Change colours: Drop first colour; with 2nd colour, pull through last 2 lps of st.

Double crochet (dc): Yo, insert hook in st, yo, pull through st, [yo, pull through 2 lps] twice.

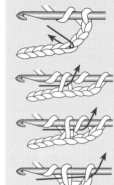

Treble crochet (tr): Yo twice, insert hook in st, yo, pull through st, [yo, pull through 2 lps] 3 times.

Single crochet decrease (sc dec): (Insert hook, yo, draw lp through) in each of the sts indicated, yo, draw through all lps on hook.

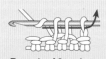

Example of 2-sc dec

Half double crochet decrease (hdc dec): (Yo, insert hook, yo, draw lp through) in each of the sts indicated, yo, draw through all lps on hook.

Example of 2-hdc dec

Double crochet decrease (dc dec): (Yo, insert hook, yo, draw loop through, draw through 2 lps on hook) in each of the sts indicated, yo, draw through all lps on hook.

Example of 2-dc dec

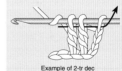

Example of 2-tr dec

Treble crochet decrease (tr dec): Holding back last lp of each st, tr in each of the sts indicated, yo, pull through all lps on hook.

US		UK
sl st (slip stitch)	=	sc (single crochet)
sc (single crochet)	=	dc (double crochet)
hdc (half double crochet)	=	htr (half treble crochet)
dc (double crochet)	=	tr (treble crochet)
tr (treble crochet)	=	dtr (double treble crochet)
dtr (double treble crochet)	=	ttr (triple treble crochet)
skip	=	miss

FEELING CRAFTY? GET CREATIVE!

Each 160-page book features easy-to-follow, step-by-step instructions and full-page colour photographs of every project. Whatever your crafting fancy, there's a Company's Coming Creative Series craft book to match!

Beading: Beautiful Accessories in Under an Hour
Complement your wardrobe, give your home extra flair or add an extra-special personal touch to gifts with these quick and easy beading projects. Create any one of these special crafts in an hour or less.

Knitting: Easy Fun for Everyone
Take a couple of needles and some yarn and see what beautiful things you can make! Learn how to make fashionable sweaters, comfy knitted blankets, scarves, bags and other knitted crafts with these easy-to-intermediate knitting patterns.

Card Making: Handmade Greetings for All Occasions
Making your own cards is a fun, creative and inexpensive way of letting someone know you care. Stamp, emboss, quill or layer designs in a creative and unique card with your own personal message for friends or family.

Patchwork Quilting
In this book full of throws, baby quilts, table toppers, wall hangings—and more—you'll find plenty of beautiful projects to try. With the modern fabrics available, and the many practical and decorative applications, patchwork quilting is not just for Grandma!

Crocheting: Easy Blankets, Throws & Wraps
Find projects perfect for decorating your home, for looking great while staying warm or for giving that one-of-a-kind gift. A range of simple but stunning designs make crocheting quick, easy and entertaining.

Sewing: Fun Weekend Projects
Find a wide assortment of easy and attractive projects to help you create practical storage solutions, decorations for any room or just the right gift for that someone special. Create table runners, placemats, baby quilts, pillows and more!